Schoolhouse

LEANNA BRODIE

TALONBOOKS

Talonbooks
P.O. Box 2076, Vancouver, British Columbia, Canada V6B 3S3
www.talonbooks.com

Typeset in New Baskerville and printed and bound in Canada.
Printed on 100% post-consumer recycled paper.

Second printing: November 2011

The publisher gratefully acknowledges the financial support of the Canada
Council for the Arts; the Government of Canada through the Book Publishing
Industry Development Program; and the Province of British Columbia
through the British Columbia Arts Council and the Book Publishing Tax
Credit for our publishing activities.

Library and Archives Canada Cataloguing in Publication

Brodie, Leanna, 1966–
        Schoolhouse / Leanna Brodie.

A play.
ISBN 978-0-88922-571-8

        I. Title.

PS8553.R6337S34 2007   C812'.6   C2007-901066-0

*This play is dedicated to
Mrs. Lander of Plainville Public School;
to her sister, Mrs. Barrett of Bewdley Public School;
and to all the good teachers.*

Schoolhouse, by Leanna Brodie, premiered on August 11, 2006 at the Blyth Festival, under the artistic direction of Eric Coates with the following cast:

MISS MELITA LINTON: Amy Jo Scherman
FLOSSIE NEEDLER, MRS. NEEDLER: Anne Anglin
RUSSELL YELLOWLEES, MR. YELLOWLEES: Clifford Cardinal
BERYL BAPTIE, MRS. BAPTIE: Ingrid Haas
EFFA BAPTIE, EVIE BOTHWELL: Marie Beath Badian
MILTON COYTE, THE GIRL, MRS. COYTE: Michelle Polak
VERN YELLOWLEES: John Munnings
DWIGHT VARNUM, MRS. VARNUM: Waawaate Fobister
EWART ROKOSH: Ian Lake
CLINTON COCHRANE, THE TEACHER,
MR. VARNUM: Kieran Gallant
COLONEL BURNETT, THE FATHER, MR. COYTE: Layne Coleman

Director: Leah Cherniak
Assistant Director: Marie Beath Badian
Set and Lighting Designer: Glenn Davidson
Costume Designer: Jennifer Triemstra
Sound Designer: Todd Charlton
Stage Manager: Giselle E. Clarke
Assistant Stage Manager: Matthew Byrne

A second production premiered at the 4th Line Theatre, under the artistic direction of Robert Winslow, on July 5, 2007 with the following cast:

MISS MELITA LINTON: Shannon Taylor
FLOSSIE NEEDLER: Jade O'Keefe
RUSSELL YELLOWLEES: Griffin Clark
BERYL BAPTIE: Emily Spasov
EFFA BAPTIE: Nora Hickey
MILTON COYTE: Cody McMahon
VERN YELLOWLEES: Anika Spasov
MR. YELLOWLEES: Mark Hiscox
DWIGHT VARNUM: Jake Vanderham
EWART ROKOSH: Will Lamond
CLINTON COCHRANE: Tim Walker
BOYD LEBEAU: Justin Hiscox
COLONEL BURNETT, MR. COYTE: Robert Winslow
EVIE BOTHWELL, MRS. COYTE: Haley McGee

THE GIRL: Christina Adams
MRS. BAPTIE: Heather Knechtel
MR. VARNUM: Peter Spasov
MRS. VARNUM: Renate Spasov
MRS. NEEDLER: Sarah Lynn Tye
Director: Kim Blackwell
Costume Designers: Angela Thomas, Kim Dooley
Set & Props Designer: Samantha Turnbull
Musical Director: Justin Hiscox
Musician: Mark Hiscox
Fight Director: Edward Belanger
Stage Manager: Sarah Lynn Tye
Assistant Stage Manager: Suzanne Leandro

CHARACTERS

MISS MELITA (*Meh-lee´-tuh*) LINTON
RUSSELL YELLOWLEES: ringleader; "Big Boy"; 14
DWIGHT VARNUM: follower; "Big Boy"; 15
EWART ROKOSH (*Roe´-kosh*): training school boy; 14
FLOSSIE NEEDLER: scrapper; 13
BERYL BAPTIE (*Bap´-tee*): future teacher; 12
MILTON COYTE: only child; 7
EFFA BAPTIE: tattletale; sister of BERYL; 8
VERN YELLOWLEES: baby of the family; brother of RUSSELL; 5
CALLUM YELLOWLEES: farmer; trustee; RUSSELL and VERN's
      father
CLINTON COCHRANE: young local man
COLONEL BURNETT: Inspector of Schools
EVIE BOTHWELL: city girl
THE GIRL: from EVIE's letter
THE FATHER: from EVIE's letter
MRS. COYTE: former teacher; MILTON's mother
EWAN COYTE: farmer; trustee; MILTON's father
ZELLAH BAPTIE: church choir leader; trustee's wife; BERYL
      and EFFA's mother
MRS. VARNUM: very near-sighted due to cataracts; DWIGHT's
      mother
LIONEL VARNUM: farmer; DWIGHT's father
MILLIE NEEDLER: farmer; widow; FLOSSIE's mother

*Diverse, non-traditional, imaginative casting is highly, strongly,
enthusiastically encouraged.*

SETTING

The play takes place in and around S.S.#1 Jericho School—
a one-room schoolhouse in a farming community near the
village of Baker's Creek—over one calendar year: January to
December, 1938.

The classroom of Jericho School, complete with blackboards,
desks, and the sempiternal wood stove; the schoolyard, with
an outhouse and possibly a shed; Baker's Creek Fairgrounds;
a small attic room with a chair; a church; the Coytes' home;
a community hall. The classroom is the primary location:
everything else need only be suggested.

ACT I

SCENE 1

The school-bell rings, and an elderly woman appears. She looks over the audience.

MISS LINTON

(*to the audience*) There was a time when I would have known everyone in this room—and all of you would have known me. Why? Because I taught you, or your children, or your children's children, that's why. Now, though, I don't know you—or if I do, I can't see you very well—and ... and I wanted to *tell* you something. So. My name is Mrs. Melita Linton Cochrane: has been for years. But my pupils from the early days still call me Miss Linton ... and that's alright by me. The thing of it is, you see, I always wanted to be a teacher. Of course, for country girls, there were only three things you could do—before you got married and your real job began. You could be a nurse; you could go to business college; or you could teach. Well, when I was a baby, I taught my dolls. When I was a girl, I taught my kittens. When I was old enough to go to school myself, I thought the years couldn't fly by fast enough: public school, high school, one year of Normal School, and I was a teacher at last! Times were hard, so it was halfway through the school year before I was offered a job. The pay was modest, and the place far from home, but none of that mattered. I was ready! Or so I thought. But we never are, are we. Ready. We're never ready for Ewart.

EWART has appeared in the background, holding a snake.

9

Oh, what am I saying, that's not where we need to start, is it.

She is transforming into her younger self.

No, we need to begin where I began: on my first day as a schoolmarm, at the ripe old age of eighteen. In January, 1938. At S.S.#1, Jericho School.

SCENE 2

Jericho School, January 1938. The children—BERYL, DWIGHT, EFFA, FLOSSIE, MILTON, and RUSSELL—are lounging around the classroom, or bouncing off the walls. Either way, the situation does not look promising. MISS LINTON, age eighteen, comes in. She seems overwhelmed by the task before her but, gathering all her strength and dignity, she strides purposefully toward the teacher's desk—and trips, or is tripped, so that she falls clumsily into it instead. The children laugh: but she manages to quiet them by ringing the handbell placed helpfully on the desk.

MISS LINTON

Good morning, class. My name is Miss Linton. Miiiss ...

She is writing it on the blackboard.

Li-n-ton. I am your teacher.

FLOSSIE

(*stage whisper*) Not for long.

The others titter. MISS LINTON whips around to face them. Silence.

MISS LINTON

Let us begin with "The Lord's Prayer."

As the others stand, close their eyes, and recite the prayer, RUSSELL sneaks over to the wood stove with a box of .22 ammunition, takes several bullets out, and chucks them into the firebox; DWIGHT sets a mouse in a drawer of the teacher's desk; and FLOSSIE places a tack on the teacher's chair. Then they tiptoe back to their desks.

ALL

... Amen.

MISS LINTON

And now for our Bible reading.

As the children resume their seats, MISS LINTON goes to the desk drawer for the Bible. When she opens the drawer, the mouse jumps out. She cries out with surprise. The children chortle delightedly.

MISS LINTON sits weakly on her chair. She yells and leaps to her feet: removes and inspects the tack; and rubs her poor punctured bum. The children hoot with pleasure. Then the shells go off inside the wood stove—pow! pow! pa-pow pow pow! ricochet ricochet ricochet—which causes the stove to shake, and MISS LINTON to shriek in alarm. She sprints over to the stove to assure herself that it is not in danger of exploding. As she makes her way back to her desk, MISS LINTON trips—or is tripped—and falls flat on her face. The children laugh themselves into fits. Then a little arm makes itself known above the desk, and tinkles its little bell. It is followed by the rest of MISS LINTON, rising and ringing her bell with more and more authority now, until the class is silent.

MISS LINTON
Good then. Now: where were we? Oh, yes.

She goes back to the desk, opens the drawer, and takes her Bible out.

Today's reading ...

RUSSELL
Hey teacher. You squealed like a girl!

MISS LINTON
Hey yourself ... *Russell Yellowlees.*

The children look at each other, startled.

I may have squealed, but I'm still here. Great-Grandpa was a Mohawk chief; my uncle fought at Wipers; and I will be here long after you're gone—for you will leave, young man: on your ear, if necessary. Do we understand each other?

Beat.

Matthew, Chapter 17: "And Jesus rebuked the devil; and he departed out of him: and the child was cured from that very hour."

(*to the audience*) Well, "cured" would be overstating the case. In the next few months, we had our ups, downs, and sideways together, but—long story short—we learned to get by. Keeping order was simple, I discovered: just work, work, work them from morn till night, and they were too busy to plot your downfall. But how to keep all the little ones and big ones on their toes at once? Rather like this:

11

SCENE 3

*March, 1938. FLOSSIE and BERYL are at the front of the class.
MISS LINTON pulls down a map of North America and indicates
the Great Lakes with her pointer. As the rest of the children are
immersed in their own activities, the girls try to best each other in
a fast-paced drill.*

MISS LINTON
The Great Lakes from west to east?

FLOSSIE
(*jumping in*) Uh, "Su—

BERYL
(*cutting her off*) —"Susan Mitchell Has Eight Oranges":
Superior, Michigan, Huron, Erie, Ontario.

MISS LINTON
The Great Lakes in order of size?

FLOSSIE
Uh, "Sam—

BERYL
—"Sam's Horse Must Eat Oats": Superior, Huron, Michigan,
Erie, Ontario.

MISS LINTON
Oceans of the world?

BERYL
"I Am A Person": Indian, Arctic, Atlantic, Pacific.

MISS LINTON
Very good, Beryl. Flossie, you must brush up your geography if
you want to get into high school. Right now, though, is your
history lesson. Quick: royal houses of England?

FLOSSIE
(*without hesitation*) "No Plan Like Yours To Study History
Wisely": Norman, Plantagenet, Lancaster, York, Tudor, Stuart,
Hanover, Windsor.

MISS LINTON
Good girl. Junior fourth: please use your book to answer these
questions on the reign of Queen Victoria. Senior third: please
solve the sums on the board. Effa and Milton: time for your
reading. Effa, will you begin with the poem on page fifteen?

EFFA

(*haltingly, as* BERYL *feeds her the words*)
"Th-r-ee li-tt-l-e, little, k-it, kit, kittens,
Lost, th-th-e-rrrr ... their ... mittens!
(*by now,* EFFA *is simply reading* BERYL's *lips*)
And they ... began ... to cry ...

BERYL AND EFFA

Very good, Effa.

MISS LINTON

Now, Beryl: it's wonderful that you taught your sister to read,
all by yourself. But it's her job to read now, and my job to help
her.

(*beat: to* EFFA) I still find it hard to believe that in all that time at
school, you never once got a lesson from your teacher.

BERYL

It's the truth, Miss Linton. Effa's always been too little to count
for much. The last one said teachers aren't judged by the
progress of the little ones. They're judged by how the Seniors
do in their entrance exams.

RUSSELL

And how good's the Christmas concert.

MISS LINTON

Russell.

(*pointing to the stove*) Wood.

RUSSELL *goes out.*

MISS LINTON

Effa: you've made really big strides in the last three months.
We'll have a look at this poem together, and I'm confident
you'll have mastered it by the end of the week. Milton: where
did we get to last time with "The Golden Touch"?

MILTON

(*declaiming quite beautifully without reference to his reader*)
"You are wiser than you were, King Midas! ... you appear to be
still capable of understanding that the commonest things, such
as lie within everybody's grasp, are more valuable than the
riches which so many mortals sigh and struggle after—"

MISS LINTON

—Milton: that is lovely, quite lovely. But you're missing one
significant part of your reading lesson:

Beat.

Reading. It is generally aided by looking at the page.

MILTON

(*sheepishly*) Oh. Yes, Teacher. Sorry.

MISS LINTON

(*to the audience*) And so on and so forth, till before you knew it, my three-ring, four-ring, six-ring circus had muddled through to Easter.

SCENE 4

Jericho School, just after Easter, 1938.

BERYL

Matthew, Chapter 28: "He is not here: for he is risen, as he said. Come, see the place where the Lord lay—"

MISS LINTON

(*to the audience*) —And that's when Mr. Yellowlees decided Vern was old enough to come to school.

An unholy sound—a sort of aria of protest—begins at a great distance and builds relentlessly as it gets closer and closer. Just at its unendurable crescendo, MR. YELLOWLEES appears on the doorstep of the classroom, carrying his screaming, squirming son, VERN. The moment VERN pauses for breath, MR. YELLOWLEES holds him out to MISS LINTON by the scruff of the neck.

MR. YELLOWLEES

He's *yours* now.

Then he deposits VERN like a bucket of slops, turns on his heel, and is gone. MISS LINTON blinks at the tantrum-riddled VERN for a moment, and looks around the classroom for inspiration. Finding it, she goes over to the desk; fetches a medicinal-looking bottle; lifts VERN firmly upright; pinches his nostrils closed so that his mouth pops open; and pours a liberal quantity directly into his mouth. He shuts up immediately, aside from a bit of spluttering.

MISS LINTON

You must be Vern. Good morning, Vern. I am Miss Linton, and *that* was cod liver oil. If you do your lessons like a Christian, you will have one spoonful of it once a day. If you fuss and fight like a savage, you will have dollops of it morning, noon, and night

14

for the rest of your miserable little life. Do we understand each other?

(*VERN nods, wide-eyed*) Good boy.

(*to the audience*) And that was pretty much that.

    Beat.

You see, the children in a country school were kind of like the actors in the Christmas play: there were only so many roles to be had, and you were a Mary or a Joseph or a Wise Man or a sheep. By this time, I thought I could handle them all. The trustees thought so, too, and by Arbour Day they'd already engaged me for another year. Then in September, just as school was about to begin, they told me I'd be getting a new pupil—a transfer—from the Battenville Training School for Boys.

SCENE 5

Jericho School, September 1938. First day of school. The children are huddled together. The bell is ringing.

THE CHILDREN
    A training school boy!

BERYL
    Ewart Rokosh.

RUSSELL
    Rokosh? What kind of a name is that!

FLOSSIE
    Wha'd'e get sent away for?

RUSSELL
    Prob'ly killed his parents.

DWIGHT
    My dad said—

VERN
    —Russell, why are the Souches taking him in?

BERYL
    Because the Souches are good Christian people, Vern.

RUSSELL
    Besides, their mule died.

MILTON
Mother says a training school boy killed his teacher.
Pause.
BERYL
That was years ago, way over in Cork County.
RUSSELL
Happens all the time. I heard about this one boy, when the
family was sleeping—
VERN starts whimpering.
RUSSELL
Aw, Vern, don't you worry about some old Battenville boy. If he
tries anything, me an' Dwight'll—
BERYL
—My cousin says last year they tried him at Bonner's School.
But he beat the tar out of Wendell Sharpe.
EFFA
Wendell Sharpe's the meanest kid in Catlow County! He weighs
eight hundred pounds!
The bell stops ringing. MISS LINTON appears.
MISS LINTON
Alright, class: it's time to start our lessons. Has anyone seen our
new boy?
EFFA
(*staring offstage*) —SNAKE!
In a trice, EWART appears, right in front of MISS LINTON—or
rather, towering over her like an overalled harbinger of doom—
holding a large and wriggly snake. Children scramble away, the
little ones shrieking in fear. MISS LINTON, however, holds her
ground. There is a slight pause.
MISS LINTON
(*valiantly struggling to appear to be calm*) You must be Ewart. Well,
Ewart, aren't you a brave boy to have found this snake and
taken it out of the playground for us. Now, you just carry it out
back and throw it across the creek so we won't need to worry
about it any longer.
(*to the rest of the class*) Would everyone please say "thank you" to
Ewart for being such a responsible, helpful boy and getting rid
of this snake for us all?

THE CHILDREN

    (*reluctantly*) Thank you, Ewart.

MISS LINTON

    Well done, class. And on your way, Ewart, you might as well take the bucket with you and get our water for the day. Class, will you please thank Ewart for fetching our water like a good, considerate boy?

THE CHILDREN

    (*same business*) Thank you, Ewart.

MISS LINTON

    Alright then: run along, now, Ewart. And when you come back, we'll all have a special lesson on herpetology: the study of snakes.

    EWART takes the snake and goes to leave with it, then swivels back, grabs the water bucket from the classroom, and heads off.

MISS LINTON

    (*to the audience*) My first test in the study of Ewart—and I seemed to have passed. For the second test, I only had to wait until recess.

SCENE 6

The schoolyard, the same day at recess. On one side of the stage, RUSSELL, FLOSSIE, and DWIGHT are tossing a ball with VERN as monkey-in-the-middle. On the other, BERYL and EFFA are playing jump-rope with MILTON as ever-ender.

EFFA AND BERYL

    (*chanting an old skipping-rhyme*)

    "I'm a little Dutch girl dressed in blue.

    Here are the things that I like to do:

    Salute to the captain, bow to the Queen

    Touch the bottom of the submarine.

    I can do the tap dance, I can do the splits.

    I can do the hokey pokey—"

    Meanwhile, EWART comes in, holding a book under his arm. RUSSELL comes and stands directly in his way. They do a little hesitation dance. Everyone else stops what they're doing to watch. RUSSELL halts.

RUSSELL
We don't want you here. Battenville boy.

DWIGHT
Jailbird.

FLOSSIE
Polak.

RUSSELL
So why don't you take your big ugly face and go back to jail.

FLOSSIE
Yeah. 'Cause your mother doesn't want you.

RUSSELL
No. 'Cause his mother's in jail, too. So go see your mother, you big ugly ape.

EWART puts the book into his pocket and takes a defensive stance. He waits. Suddenly, EFFA rockets off towards the classroom. With a war cry, RUSSELL launches himself at EWART. EWART neatly trips RUSSELL so that he goes flying into the dust hard enough to knock the wind out of him. DWIGHT and FLOSSIE, seeing that RUSSELL is down for the count, go for EWART. He puts them down, too— effortlessly and bloodlessly. MISS LINTON's whistle is heard: everyone except EWART scrambles into a line; and EFFA comes back on, followed by MISS LINTON.

MISS LINTON
What happened here?

Pause.

Have you been fighting?

Pause.

I want the truth.

Beat.

EWART
Yes, Miss, the truth. I was comin' back from a walk to the creek. These kids were playin' ball. The girls were doin' jump-rope. I stopped for a rest. We had a little talk.

MILTON
I'm not a girl!

BERYL
Hush, Milton.

MISS LINTON
    And is that what really happened?

RUSSELL
    Yes, Teacher. That's what happened alright.

FLOSSIE
    Cross my heart. Hope to die.

DWIGHT
    No fightin', that's for sure.

MISS LINTON
    Well. Ewart, I'm glad you remember that it is your Christian
    duty to show patience and forbearance with those who are not
    as big and strong as you are. And speaking of our Christian
    duty, I'm also glad that everyone is making Ewart feel welcome
    on his first day in a new school. Now: I believe recess is over.
    (*as they file past her into the school*) I think I have our Bible
    reading picked out for tomorrow. Hebrews 13:2, "Be not
    forgetful to entertain strangers: for thereby some have
    entertained angels unawares ... "

SCENE 7

Jericho School, September 1938.

MISS LINTON
    Junior Fourth: come to the front, please.
        RUSSELL and EWART shuffle forward.

MISS LINTON
    (*to the audience*) A couple of weeks later, it was time to take up
    Russell and Ewart's recitations. Russell, of course, chose the
    kind of piece that has been beloved of schoolboys for a
    thousand years.

RUSSELL
    " ... Cannon to right of them,
    Cannon to left of them,
    Cannon in front of them
    Volley'd and thundered,
    Stormed at with ... Stormed at with ... "
    Uh ...
        He is lost.

19

MISS LINTON

Russell, I'm sure Tennyson himself would applaud your patriotic spirit—and excellent phrasing. However, just like the Light Brigade itself, you need to make it to the end of the Charge. Please look over the poem and we'll try again.

RUSSELL

Yes, Teacher.

MISS LINTON

Now: Ewart?

EWART shifts uncomfortably.

MISS LINTON

Ewart, did you not prepare a recitation?

EWART

Yes, Miss. I was wonderin', Miss. Do I hafta say it out loud?

MISS LINTON

Well, Ewart, that is generally the point of a recitation.

. *The class laughs.*

MISS LINTON

Quiet, everyone. Go ahead, Ewart. Please.

After another pause, he begins.

EWART

"What if I say I shall not wait?
What if I burst the fleshly gate
And pass, escaped, to thee? ... "

He hesitates.

RUSSELL

Well, that's some fleshy gate he's got there. If he bursts that, it'll be one heck of a mess.

The class laughs.

MISS LINTON

CLASS! That's enough!

Beat.

Go on, Ewart.

EWART

(*uncomfortable*) Please, Miss, I'd rather not ...

MISS LINTON

But I'd rather you did. I would really like to hear the rest of that poem.

EWART

>(*after a moment*)
>
>"What if I say I shall not wait?
>What if I burst the fleshly gate
>And pass, escaped, to thee?
>What if I file this mortal off,
>See where it hurt me,—that's enough,—
>And wade in liberty?
>They cannot take me any more ... "
>
>>*Beat.*
>
>"They cannot take me any more ... "
>
>>*Beat.*
>
>I'm sorry, Miss. I ... I can't.
>
>>*Pause.*

MISS LINTON

>Ewart, that was ... that was very good, as far as it went. But you, too, must be prepared to do the whole poem next time.

EWART

>Yes, Miss.

MISS LINTON

>(*to the audience*) All that day, I was haunted by Ewart's recitation. And the day came to an end.
>
>(*to class*) Class dismissed!
>
>>*The class heads out to the cloakroom.*

MISS LINTON

>Ewart ...
>
>>*EWART turns back.*

MISS LINTON

>That poem. It's not from your reader. It's not in our little bookshelf.
>
>>*Beat.*
>
>What is it?

EWART

>It's by ... Emily Dickinson. It was in this book from ... from Battenville School.
>
>>*He fishes a small bound volume from his pocket.*
>
>I still read it a lot.

MISS LINTON
    Huh. Ewart, what do you think the poem is about?
EWART
    It's about … hurtin', I guess. Bein' … so lonesome you could …
        He trails off.
MISS LINTON
    Yes.
EWART
    (*beat*) Is that it, Miss? They'll be wantin' me for the chores.
MISS LINTON
    Of course. No, Ewart, you go on home.
        EWART leaves.
MISS LINTON
    … wherever that may be.

SCENE 8

The schoolyard. The children are playing Anti-I-Over around the woodshed or outhouse. One team consists of RUSSELL, FLOSSIE, MILTON, and VERN.

FLOSSIE

ANTI-I-OVER!

She throws the ball over the roof. Seconds later, the opposing team—BERYL, EFFA, and DWIGHT—springs a classic Anti-I-Over attack, hurtling around both sides of the building at once, and screaming like banshees all the while. BERYL, who is "it", manages to tag MILTON before the others disappear to the other side of the building.

As she is about to throw the ball over the roof, BERYL stops herself and hands it to MILTON.

BERYL

Go on, Milton, you throw it. Need some help?

MILTON

(*looking off into the distance*) Where's Ewart?

RUSSELL

(*offstage voice*) Hey! Get the lead out over there!

EFFA
C'mon, Milton. They're waiting.

MILTON
Everyone's mean to him.

BERYL
Nobody's mean to Ewart, Milton. We just leave him alone.

RUSSELL
(*offstage voice*) What's going on over there? You didn't give the ball to Milton, did you?

DWIGHT
C'mon, Milton.

MILTON
ANTI-I-OVER!

He throws the ball over the roof: seconds later, RUSSELL, FLOSSIE, and VERN appear; but they are doing the casual, who's-got-that-ball variation of Anti-I-Over strategy, until RUSSELL springs the attack ... and snags MILTON. BERYL, DWIGHT, and EFFA, meanwhile, peel back around the building to safety.

BERYL
(*as she disappears*) Aw. He got Milton. Again.

RUSSELL
ANTI-I-OVER!

He whips the ball over the roof ... and there is the sound of breaking glass. FLOSSIE, VERN, and RUSSELL run off in the direction of the noise. After a moment, RUSSELL runs back onstage, and the other children come and crowd around him.

FLOSSIE
Boy, you're in for it now.

MILTON reappears and goes tearing off toward the school.

VERN
Russell, that man's gonna be mad you broke his truck. We should go hide.

RUSSELL
(*nervously*) I'm not scared. You go hide. Me and Dwight'll—

OFFSTAGE VOICE
(*thunderous and male*) WHO THREW THAT BALL?

The children look at each other.

BERYL

Don't worry, Russell, we'll stand by you. We'll—

EFFA

IT WAS RUSSELL YELLOWLEES.

RUSSELL

Shut up, simp.

OFFSTAGE VOICE

COME HERE, RUSS.

Nobody moves.

OFFSTAGE VOICE

ALRIGHT: I'M COMING THERE. I HAVE SOMETHING FOR YOU.

CLINTON COCHRANE enters from upstage. He is an impressive-looking figure in his twenties, with great charm and a certain natural authority, dressed in rubber boots and overalls, and carrying a dirty old ball.

CLINTON

Now, which one of you little hooligans is Russ?

He looks sternly at all the children in turn. EFFA manages to convey RUSSELL's whereabouts to CLINTON without getting caught.

CLINTON

(*going to RUSSELL*) I believe this is yours?

RUSSELL

I ... I ... yeah.

CLINTON

"Yeah"? "Yeah"?

RUSSELL

Yeah—I mean, yes.

CLINTON

"Yes" what?

RUSSELL

Oh. Yes, sir.

CLINTON

Yes, sir. That is correct. Now, do you hooligans have a teacher?

MISS LINTON enters rapidly with MILTON in tow.

MISS LINTON

What seems to be the problem, sir.

CLINTON

Oh, nothing much. Just the two dollars I'm going to extract from Russ's hide to pay for my broken side window.

MISS LINTON

The young man does not have two dollars, but I'm sure we can work something out that will satisfy you. He did not mean to damage your truck, after all: they were only playing Anti-I-Over.

CLINTON

Anti-I-Over?

MISS LINTON

You must have played it. Alley-Alley-Over ... Olly-Olly-Over ... Auntie-Over-Shanty ...

CLINTON

I know what it is. I just don't know how it's going to fix my truck.

MISS LINTON

And I'm very sorry about that, sir ... however, you will not need to take anything out of Russell's hide. I do not allow corporal punishment in my school.

CLINTON

YOUR school? You mean they let a little girl like you run a school, all by yourself? Well, that explains why grown men like these are running amok in a schoolyard these days, instead of helping out with the harvest like every useful man in this county. These boys must be sweet on you.

MISS LINTON

(*to the children*) Lunchtime is over, children. Go inside.

The children head off.

BERYL

Come on, everyone. It's almost time for music class. Vern, don't wipe your nose on your sleeve when I know very well you've got a hankie in your pocket.

They are gone.

MISS LINTON

Mister ... ? I am sorry, I have not had the pleasure of an introduction.

CLINTON

Clinton Cochrane.

MISS LINTON

… And now, I have still not had the *pleasure* of an introduction. Whoever you are, you have no call to speak to me in front of the children like that. It is widely considered that I am one of the best teachers in the history of Jericho School. And no hayseed bully in his rusty jalopy has the right to come in here and sneer at that, not for five dozen side windows.

CLINTON

Hayseed bully?!

He takes a step or two toward MISS LINTON … when EWART appears, replacing his book in his pocket, and stubbing out a cigarette.

EWART

Wouldn't go no further, if I was you.

(*to MISS LINTON*) Sorry, Miss. Went down to the creek to smoke my cigarette. Out of respect.

MISS LINTON

Well, I appreciate your delicacy, Ewart, but we are going to have a little talk about the effects of tobacco on hygiene. Now run along inside and get ready for your music lesson.

(*EWART hesitates*) Run along.

He leaves. CLINTON looks after him in awe.

CLINTON

You mean to tell me THAT is your pupil?

MISS LINTON

Ewart is not a "that." He is a bright and sensitive boy.

CLINTON

Well whatever you call him, you seem to manage him pretty well. And no strap?

(*shakes his head*) There's more to you than meets the eye. Not that there's anything wrong with what meets the eye. But you are a firecracker. 'Course, the Hoopers that you're boarding with, they're my second cousins, and the Hooper boys say you're too stuck-up to date the local fellows. Shame about that.

MISS LINTON

The Hooper boys—

(*realising*) If you were driving down the road, how did Russell manage to break your … Mister Cochrane. Were you by any chance *parked* outside this school at the time you got hit? Were you, in fact, stopping by just to have a look at the new teacher?

CLINTON

(*smiling*) Oh, you're not new, Miss Linton. With the turnaround on this school, you're a grizzled veteran. Good afternoon.

He goes out.

MISS LINTON

(*after a moment*) FINE, THEN! THAT'S FINE! ... AND YOU CAN FIX YOUR OWN BLESSED TRUCK!

SCENE 9

Jericho School, October 1938. A piano plays a wicked jazz lick, segueing into the introduction to "The Maple Leaf Forever," and a choir of children joins in. MISS LINTON listens for a moment.

MISS LINTON

(*to the audience*) Ah, Boyd Lebeau. Best music teacher in Cork, Catlow, or any county at all. Best jazz musician west of Montreal, they say. Best drinker, too, unfortunately. Though of course not in front of the children. They loved him, naturally. He always said: "Melita, with music, you can get the little ones to do almost anything for you." Of course, it didn't hurt that he could also pull out his medals and his shell casings and get them all saucer-eyed with tales of Vimy Ridge.

Boyd does a little ragtime riff.

Oh, Boyd.

(*to the audience*) I loved that old piano. Of course, you couldn't teach a classroom full of kids how to play the one piano, so Boyd made them all get Attaboy mouth organs, twenty-five cents a go. They sure made a splash at the school fair.

SCENE 10

Baker's Creek Fairgrounds, October 1938. To the boom-boom-boom of a drum, the whole student body of Jericho School—in drill formation—comes marching into sight. They are all adorned with a sash in the school colours. BERYL looks proud as punch as she holds the school flag. RUSSELL courts deafness with a big bass drum. All the others are playing a verse of the school song on their mouth organs. As they reach the centre, MISS LINTON blows her whistle and they begin to march on the spot, singing the school yell:

THE CHILDREN OF JERICHO
Well we don't have trumpets but we make a sound,
And all the other schools come tumbling down,
O Jericho, Jericho,
S.S. #1!
We are the best, put us to the test,
Always number one—what fun!

MISS LINTON
Very good, class!

LOUDSPEAKER VOICE
Attention, students. The Catlow County Parade of Schools will begin by the bleachers at eleven o'clock. That's fifteen minutes to the Parade.

MISS LINTON
Alright: that gives us time to go look at the entries for the garden competition. But you must all be back here ready to go when that big clock shows eleven: is that understood?

THE CHILDREN OF JERICHO
Yes, Miss Linton.

MISS LINTON
Good. Colonel Burnett does not brook lateness: and neither do I.
(*looking off*) Well, speak of the devil ... CLASS! Atten-TION!
Enter COLONEL BURNETT, a small man in a large helmet, sporting full military dress, with an impressive display of medals on his chest.

MISS LINTON
Class, what do we say to the Inspector of Schools?

THE CHILDREN OF JERICHO
Good morning, Colonel Burnett.

COLONEL BURNETT
Troops! Hands out front!

MISS LINTON

Oh, Colonel, I had just told the children they could go and look at the—

COLONEL BURNETT

HANDS OUT FRONT! Can't see your company's hair and fingernails from the reviewing stand, can I? Not going to give the prize to a troop that marches well but can't clean its weapons, am I?

MISS LINTON

Well ... children, let's just take a minute then.

COLONEL BURNETT

(*inspecting the proffered fingernails*) Good. Good. Good. Good.

(*he comes to EWART*) Good Lord. What in the Sam Hill is this?

MISS LINTON

This is Ewart. He is one of my best students.

COLONEL BURNETT

I should say so, at his age. Young man, why are you not in uniform?

EWART

There isn't a war on. Sir.

COLONEL BURNETT

Well we'll just see about that.

MISS LINTON

He's fourteen, Colonel.

COLONEL BURNETT

Good gravyboats! Fourteen. I always said the most impressive soldiers are farmboys.

MISS LINTON

Begging your pardon, Colonel, Ewart is not really a—

COLONEL BURNETT

—Oh, yes: this is your training school boy, isn't it? Sent down for farm work after you'd served your time in the brig, were you, boy? So what did you do, anyway?

EWART doesn't answer.

No matter, no matter: there's nothing like the discipline of the plough to straighten out those youthful high spirits. I'm sure the Souch farm will make a man out of you—and if not, there's always the Army, eh, boy?

EWART

The Army? The Army's the last thing—

MISS LINTON

(*jumping in*) —Colonel. I was wondering if you had a moment, because, I've, been reading that book on school management you left me at last year's inspection, and there's a passage on which I could use your elucidation.

COLONEL BURNETT

Elucidation, Miss Linton! I'd be delighted.

(*to the children*) COMPANY! Fall out!

They disappear gratefully to the four winds.

MISS LINTON

Now, let me just see if—I'm almost sure I brought it with me, just in case ...

She fumbles for it in her satchel, as CLINTON COCHRANE appears. This time, he is dressed in a suit, with neat hair and a clipboard.

COLONEL BURNETT

Ah, Clinton my lad! How goes it with the field-crops of battle?

CLINTON

Hello, Tom. Fine, thanks. It's actually kind of embarrassing the way people treat me like a war hero just because I went away and got a piece of paper. And I don't see how it makes me qualified to judge some schoolkid's pumpkins.

(*seeing MISS LINTON*) Oh. Hello.

COLONEL BURNETT

Come on, lad. It's not every day a Baker's Creek boy gets his engineer's degree. They're proud of you.

MISS LINTON

Hello.

COLONEL BURNETT

Say—you two already know each other? My, you college boys move fast.

MISS LINTON

I thought you were a farmer, Mr. Cochrane.

CLINTON

Never said I was, Miss Linton.

COLONEL BURNETT

Fine farming family, the Cochranes. Clinton's the first one to be a suit-and-tie man, aren't you, lad?

MISS LINTON
     If you gentlemen will excuse me, I should go and keep an eye
     on my children.
CLINTON
     I can give you a hand, if you'd like.
MISS LINTON
     Oh, no, Mr. Cochrane. I'd never ask you to do my job for me.
     You see, even a little girl like me can sometimes run a school
     all by herself. Especially when she's a grizzled veteran. Good
     day.
          She moves off.
COLONEL BURNETT
     My lad, I didn't understand a word of that, but I would say that
     you have just been sassed.
CLINTON
     Yes, Uncle: I have.
          They leave.
LOUDSPEAKER VOICE
     Attention students: the Public Speaking Contest will begin at
     three o'clock in the big tent. That's five minutes to the Public
     Speaking Contest.
MISS LINTON
     (*to the audience*) For those of us who taught in little country
     schools, the best thing about the school fair was the chance to
     see our fellow teachers. And after a long hot afternoon, no one
     could liven up your day like my Normal School chum, Evie
     Bothwell.
          EVIE, a stylish teenager, appears with a cigarette.
EVIE
     Hide me.
MISS LINTON
     EVIE! There are people everywhere!
EVIE
     That's the point of saying "hide me."
MISS LINTON
     (*looking around nervously as EVIE lights up*) I can't believe you
     kept up that filthy habit. What a poor example for the
     children.

31

EVIE

Knock it off, Lita. I was your roommate, see. You may come over all holy in the daylight, but you fart in your sleep like the rest of us.

MISS LINTON

I'm going to smell like smoke.

EVIE

Then stay upwind.

(*she smokes*) It's either this or my flask. It'll soon be time to gather up the little bastards, and I'm not doing that without a wee pick-me-up.

MISS LINTON

You don't sound very grateful to have a job at a time like this.

EVIE

Aw, save it, sister. I work like a mutt for these ungrateful kids, and I make less than spit for it. I go months without seeing the inside of a picture-show. I don't see anyone except snot-nosed brats, scowling parents, prying landlords—and the whole gang of them smells like cow.

> *Beat.*

Honestly, doesn't it ever make you want to ... kick over the traces a little?

MISS LINTON

That's the difference between you and me, Evie. I don't notice the traces.

> *EVIE smokes in silence for a moment.*

EVIE

So I heard you just got stuck with a training school boy. Hard luck. What'd he do, anyway? Knife his mother? Or maybe he was a rum-runner!

MISS LINTON

I don't know.

EVIE

You don't know? How can you not know?

MISS LINTON

Oh, come on, Evie, he didn't murder his mother. You know very well they only put the good ones on the farms, the ones that deserve a chance, because ... well, because some people, unlike you, think that country life builds character. Anyway, I

don't want to look at him every day and see—whatever he did.
I just want to see a boy and teach him.

Beat.

... And he's a little young to have been a rum-runner.

EVIE

Okay: live in ignorance, then. But you do think about it, all the
same. I know you.

Beat.

Oh, well. You just watch out for him, anyway. They've got an
anger in them, those kids, and if they didn't have it when they
went to training school, they sure have it after. You know what
everyone says about those places, don't you?

(*a stage whisper*) Don't drop your soap in the showers.

She laughs. MISS LINTON looks bewildered.

MISS LINTON

Why ever not?

EVIE

Oh, Lita. You really are a country girl!

She stubs out her smoke and checks the big clock.

Look at that: four o'clock. Time to round up my little buggers.
Those stupid green sashes should help. See you, Melita.

MISS LINTON

See you, Evie.

... And she is gone.

LOUDSPEAKER VOICE

Attention students: it is now four o'clock. Please retrieve your
exhibits and meet your teachers for your ride home. Would
Beryl Baptie and Lorne Howson please report to the big tent.

*Meanwhile, the children troop in, carrying their various exhibits:
DWIGHT has a dairy calf, and a handmade milk stool; RUSSELL
has a barley sheaf and mangels; they have various ribbons between
them. RUSSELL is counting his prize money.*

RUSSELL

Forty-two ... forty-five ... fifty. Hey, Teacher! I won fifty cents for
my barley sheaf and mangels!

MISS LINTON

Good for you, Russell.

DWIGHT

Hey, Russell. Give you two cents if my calf can eat your
mangels.

RUSSELL

... That's fifty-two cents! Holy jumpin', I wish I'd gotten into
this racket sooner. I would've had a BB gun by now.

*They gather round MISS LINTON and begin to show her their
winnings. Meanwhile, on the opposite side of the stage, MILTON
comes in purposefully with a tall, lovely flowering plant; a
beautiful new book tied in a ribbon; and FLOSSIE and EFFA
buzzing around him.*

FLOSSIE

Aw, come on, Milton.

EFFA

Please, Milton.

MILTON

(*stopping*) No. I am not going to share my prize book with you,
and do you know why? When Teacher gave out the flower seeds
for the school fair, you two picked zinnias and asters, just like
everyone else. Asters and zinnias, zinnias and asters. I was the
only one who picked salpiglossis, and you all made fun. All I
ever heard was, "Salpiglossis, salpiglossis, Milton with his
salpiglossis. Hey, Milton got his tonsils out: he has salpiglossis!"
Well, comes the school fair, and guess what? Your zinnias and
asters are up against umpteen dozen from all around the
township, and they're all better than yours because you never
did fertilise the roots, did you?

FLOSSIE

Lookit, brown-nose, we got better things to—

MILTON

—And meanwhile I have the nicest salpiglossis in Catlow
County, and I have a brand-new Gene Stratton-Porter book,
and you have goose eggs and a raspberry.

... And he blows one at them.

FLOSSIE

Aw, Milton, your mother's got all kinds of books. We never get
nothin' new to read. I read every book in that darn bookcase
twice already, and Gene Stratton-Porter is my favourite.

EFFA

Pretty-please with sugar on top, Milton. Miss Linton says you're supposed to share.

MILTON

Oh yeah? What about when I had the mumps and I begged someone to water my salpiglossis and nobody would?

Beat.

Well, remember what the Little Red Hen said? "You would not help me sow the grain. You would not help me water the grain. You would not help me reap the grain. So I will eat it myself." Now leave me alone.

MISS LINTON

Flossie! Effa! Milton! Come and gather round! Mr. Yellowlees is going to be coming any minute, and we don't want to keep him waiting!

EWART comes in empty-handed.

MISS LINTON

Ewart! Where's your drawing?

EWART

Oh, I didn't bother about that, Miss.

MISS LINTON

Well, go and get it—hurry. Our ride will be here.

EWART

It's alright, Miss. I'm not much of a drawer. I only did it 'cause I didn't have time to grow nothin' or build nothin'. I didn't win a prize, anyway.

MISS LINTON

The point is, Ewart, you did your best. That's what this fair is about, class. It's not about the winning and losing, it's about the—

RUSSELL

—Holy Queen of Sheba.

... And BERYL comes in. She is a sight to behold, arms full of ribbons, trundling a little wagon full of her entries in every conceivable class. She is carrying a book tied up in a ribbon like MILTON's, and a large silver cup. VERN is helping her.

BERYL

Sorry I'm late.

The children crowd around to inspect her haul.

FLOSSIE
    I wish they didn't have classes that are just for boys. It's no fair.
    I could make a better milking stool than Dwight.

RUSSELL
    Why—because you're such a cow?

        FLOSSIE goes for RUSSELL. MISS LINTON intervenes.

MISS LINTON
    CLASS! I am certain we are all proud of Beryl's
    accomplishments—

        A farm truck is heard honking.

RUSSELL AND VERN
    There's Dad!

MISS LINTON
    Off we go, children.

        *They are already heading out toward the truck, EWART lagging
        behind.*

MISS LINTON
    Ewart, I want to put up your drawing at the front of the class
    this month. I think it's beautiful. So run along and get it,
    Ewart. Go.

EWART
    (*his face brightening*) Yes, Miss.

        *MISS LINTON follows the children toward the truck, and EWART
        runs back to the fair.*

SCENE 11

*Jericho schoolyard, October 31, 1938. FLOSSIE, RUSSELL, and
DWIGHT come running out to the outhouse.*

FLOSSIE
    ... So, what are we gonna do first? Are we gonna tip over the
    outhouse? It don't feel like Hallowe'en if you boys don't tip
    over the outhouse.

RUSSELL
    Are you crazy? It's broad daylight. We'll come back tonight and
    tip it over. Right now, we're doin' somethin' better.

FLOSSIE
    Like what?

RUSSELL
You know Dwight helps his dad with butcherin' the steers.

FLOSSIE
Yeah.

RUSSELL
So, where do you think we put the biggest, meanest, blood-drippin' steer's head?

They indicate the outhouse door. They laugh.

FLOSSIE
Say, who do you think is in for it?

DWIGHT
Milton.

RUSSELL
Milton, of course. It'll be a scream.

DWIGHT
The bookworm.

FLOSSIE
He's such a little weirdie.

RUSSELL
He's such a little baby.

DWIGHT
He always comes for to take a wee.

RUSSELL
Right at the end of the school day.

DWIGHT
And he's just the right height.

RUSSELL
When he opens the door, he'll be smack-dab at eye level.

DWIGHT
And there's Mr. Steer's Head sayin' how-de-do.

They laugh.

FLOSSIE
You boys are dogs.

RUSSELL
Sshh. Here he comes.

They hide behind the outhouse. MILTON comes on, opens the door, and screams. FLOSSIE, RUSSELL, and DWIGHT dash out, chuck MILTON into the outhouse, and lock the door. MILTON starts banging frantically on the door, screaming and hollering. His three tormentors fall about laughing. EFFA appears, sizes up the situation, and takes off toward the school. Then EWART comes running from the direction of the creek. He looks at the scene, puts away his book, and starts toward the perpetrators.

RUSSELL

You gonna take us on, jailbird? We ain't afraid of you. Why, me and Dwight'll—

EWART cold-cocks him. RUSSELL, though stunned, manages to get back up and take off, with FLOSSIE and DWIGHT in hot pursuit. EWART follows them and there are sounds of a brief melée followed by moaning and groaning. EWART walks back into sight without a scratch on him. He frees MILTON, who is crying pitiably. MILTON throws his arms around the legs of EWART, who tries awkwardly to detach himself.

EWART

There. Okay, now. Okay. Yer alright. Yer alright.

MISS LINTON

(*offstage*) Russell! Dwight! Flossie! You come back here RIGHT NOW!

But instead, the three pranksters rocket off into the Hallowe'en horizon. EWART tries to escape as well, but MILTON is still holding on to him. After a moment of internal struggle, he leans down to MILTON.

EWART

Hey. You want to go see Teacher?

MILTON, still sobbing, nods solemnly.

EWART

Okay, then. Here we go.

He offers MILTON his hand, and they go off toward the schoolhouse.

SCENE 12

Jericho School, November 1, 1938. MISS LINTON stands in front of the line of defendants: EWART, DWIGHT, FLOSSIE, and RUSSELL. The latter three are bandaged, plastered, and bruised. Silence.

MISS LINTON

Now. Who has an explanation as to why you three saw fit to
lock a seven-year-old boy in the privy with a freshly butchered
cow?

DWIGHT

Well, Dad told me for to go do somethin' with the head.

*RUSSELL and FLOSSIE snicker, but MISS LINTON withers them with
a look.*

MISS LINTON

Let's try this again. Who has an *intelligent* explanation?

RUSSELL

It was just Hallowe'en, Teacher. We was just trying to scare him.
It was all in fun.

MISS LINTON

Oh, good, Russell, I'm glad you explained that you were trying
to scare him, because if I thought you were trying to behave
like decent young people, I would be confused.

Beat—she changes tone completely.

By the way, Dwight, how's your calf?

DWIGHT

(*startled*) Do you mean me, Teacher?

MISS LINTON

Yes, I do. Your calf that we saw at the school fair. That was a
fine-looking animal—how's she doing?

DWIGHT

Well, Teacher, she's doing alright ... Now, mind, she was
stamping pretty good after the fair—I thought she might have
the water belly. So, that Mond'y I upped her salt and watched
her all night for to see if she kicked her stomach and whatnot,
but turns out she was just itchin' the muskittuhs.

MISS LINTON

Dwight Varnum, I suspect that is the most you have ever said at
one time in your life. Now why would you take such care with a
dairy calf? Do you love this calf? Is she a friend, would you say?

DWIGHT

I don't know, Teacher. You can't keep no cattle as a friend, it
don't work out too good. Still, I raised her up pretty good, I
guess, and she's a good little calf. I guess I feel all tied up with
her.

MISS LINTON
So, you feel all tied up with minding a defenceless little beast but not with minding a defenceless little boy who needs your protection at least as much as that calf does?

Beat.

You three don't like Milton, and there's not a blessed thing I can do about it. But you should know by now that someone smaller and frailer than you is someone you're supposed to look out for—the way the older children once looked out for you. So: today, at the end of class, I will escort you home to your parents, to tell them why you are suspended for one week.

There is consternation amongst the children.

MISS LINTON
Milton was banging on that door so hard his little hands are bruised purple. His mother says he cried himself to sleep. Perhaps when you are home reflecting on your actions, you will find it in your hearts to be ashamed.

(*turning to EWART*) Now, as for you, Ewart: I appreciate that you rescued Milton and brought him to me. I would just like to get something straight. When you came up from the creek, you saw … ?

EWART
Russell and them rollin' around laughin'. And I heard Milton in the outhouse.

MISS LINTON
And then?

EWART
I went for Russell and I hit him. Then I chased them around back and we went at it pretty good.

FLOSSIE
He—

MISS LINTON
—Quiet, Flossie. Yes, Ewart, I can see how "good" you went at it. And then?

EWART
Then I come around and let Milton out.

MISS LINTON
I see.

Beat.

Were you surprised that you could fend these three off so easily? Did you think at the time they would be able to stop you?

EWART

Oh, no, Miss. They couldn'a stopped me.

MISS LINTON

… Which means they couldn't have stopped you if you had marched right over and opened the outhouse door?

Beat.

Instead of which, you let Milton spend a few more minutes with a severed head for company while you meted out cowboy justice. Do I strike you as an incompetent person, Ewart?

EWART

No, Miss, no …

MISS LINTON

Then why did you think that giving out punishment in this school was your job instead of mine?

Pause.

EWART

I guess I wasn't thinkin' like that, Miss. I just saw them laughin' and heard him scream and … then I guess I wasn't thinkin' nothin' at all.

MISS LINTON

I see.

Beat.

Ewart, you are suspended for two days. I will be taking you home to Souch's farm to explain what happened.

EWART

(*very agitated*) Oh, no, please, Miss, you—

Beat—then a monotone.

Yes, Miss. Whatever you say.

MISS LINTON

Good. Now then: I am assigning all of you a composition during your time away. You are to write a fairy tale or fable that will teach something to the little ones. Perhaps it will even awaken in you some sense of duty. Dismissed.

The children leave the school. FLOSSIE, RUSSELL, and DWIGHT
appear separately with pencils and scribblers. They are at home
working on their stories.

FLOSSIE

Once upon a time ...

DWIGHT

Once ... upon ... a ...

RUSSELL

Once upon a time, there was a—

SCENE 13

Jericho School, November 4, 1938. EWART appears.

EWART

Once upon a time there was a big giant boy with a scary face.
And everyone was afraid of him. But he wasn't always so big.
Before, he was a Little Little Boy, who was afraid of everyone
else. He was afraid of his reflection in the mirror. He was afraid
of his shadow on the ground. Mostly, he was afraid of the Big
People. The Big People were everywhere. All day, they moved
the Small People from room to room. In every room they
shouted at them because they did something wrong. But
sometimes Big People were really ... nice ... to the Little Little
Boy. Sometimes, they shared ... secrets ... with the Little Little
Boy, and afterwards, they gave him special treats. What he
didn't know was that there was a magic curse inside the treats.
The curse was that if you took the treats, it left a mark on your
forehead like a silver star.

   Beat.

One day the Big People sent the Little Little Boy away, and he
was so happy. But what he didn't know was there would always
be Big People and they would always be able to see his silver
scar if they knew where to look. The end.

MISS LINTON

(*to the audience*) That day I kept Ewart after class.

(*to EWART*) Silver scar.

EWART

Yes, Miss?

MISS LINTON

> At first you wrote that the boy had a silver star on his forehead. Then you wrote, "silver scar."

EWART

> Sorry, Miss. I'll fix it.

MISS LINTON

> I don't think that's what needs fixing, Ewart. I think the story's not finished. I think there's more.

EWART

> No, Miss. That's the whole story, alright.

MISS LINTON

> Well, it's not good enough. The assignment was to use a fable to impart a lesson to the little ones. What is the lesson you are teaching here?
>
> *Beat.*

EWART

> I guess they should stick with it and things will turn out alright. I only had two days to write this, Miss. I'm sorry if it's not very good.
>
> *Beat.*

MISS LINTON

> Ewart, did all of the Small People have scars on their foreheads? Or was it only the Little Little Boy?

EWART

> I don't know. It's a secret.
>
> (*beat—very abruptly*) I gotta go.

MISS LINTON

> Ewart, I am only trying to understand your story. So what can you tell me that will help me understand?
>
> *Beat—she reads from his story:*
>
> "Sometimes Big People were really nice to the Little Little Boy" ... why? Why did they give him treats? When you say the Big People shared "secrets" with the Little Little Boy ... what kind of secrets?
>
> (*beat*) Ewart ...

EWART

> I'm sorry, Miss. I really gotta go.
>
> *He leaves. She looks after him.*

SCENE 14

Jericho School, end of November, 1938. Class is in session. EWART is absent.

MISS LINTON

(*to the audience*) One thing you can say about a schoolteacher's life: there's no time to brood.

VERN

Teacher, Teacher, Teacher, Teacher!

MISS LINTON

Yes, what is it, Vern?

VERN

Look at my tooth!

MISS LINTON studies it seriously.

MISS LINTON

Yes, Vern. That is one very loose tooth.

VERN beams.

MISS LINTON

Alright, everyone. It's time to clear these desks away and rehearse for the Christmas concert. Let's start with the drill.

The children proceed to clear the desks.

RUSSELL

(*to DWIGHT*) Oh, no. Not the drill.

BERYL

We can't do the drill, Miss Linton. Ewart's away.

RUSSELL

(*quickly, to MISS LINTON*) That's right, Teacher, he's not here.

MILTON

I can't practise without Ewart. He's my partner.

MISS LINTON

Milton, you're a very clever boy and I'm sure you can imagine Ewart is there, can't you.

MILTON

Yes, Teacher.

With MISS LINTON playing a stirring march on the piano, they are meant to go through a patriotic drill, complete with flags. However, the first attempt rapidly turns into a train wreck.

44

MISS LINTON
Alright, what happened?

EFFA
It's Vern's fault, Miss Linton.

BERYL
Effa, don't tattle.

(*to MISS LINTON*) It was, though. Vern followed his brother instead of splitting to the right.

RUSSELL
Prob'ly didn't want to stand behind Flossie.

MISS LINTON
Russell. Now, let's try that one more time.

This time through, MILTON whacks RUSSELL in the head with a flag standard.

RUSSELL
Ow! Watch it, you little—

The others cluster around him.

MILTON
(*running out*) I'm sorry. I'm sorry.

BERYL
Oh, he didn't hit you that hard. Leave him alone, you big crybaby.

RUSSELL
Am not, Bossy Beryl.

MISS LINTON
That's enough, you two. Russell, are you hurt at all? Let me see.

VERN
Russell, your face is busted.

MISS LINTON
Nonsense, Vern: it's just a little nosebleed. Beryl, go and get the Junior Red Cross kit.

BERYL
Yes, Miss Linton.

As BERYL and the others ply their craft on RUSSELL with the Junior Red Cross kit, MISS LINTON turns to the audience.

MISS LINTON
Yes, Friday afternoons in November meant either the Christmas concert, or Junior Red Cross. Or occasionally, both at once.

(*to the children*) Class dismissed!

The class goes out.

THE CHILDREN

(*variously*) 'Bye, Teacher. See you Monday, Teacher. Good-bye, Miss Linton.

MISS LINTON

(*simultaneously*) Good-bye. Have a good weekend.

MISS LINTON goes to her desk and sits heavily for a moment. She takes an envelope from her satchel, and looks at the letter inside. EVIE appears.

EVIE AND MISS LINTON

Dear Melita;

I don't know why I'm telling you this: it's not like there's anything you can do. But there's this girl in my class who is subject to the fits.

THE GIRL appears, reading, and humming to herself.

EVIE

It's been going on for months, more and more. From twice a week to twice a day; three times a day; four times a day. I went to see the family.

THE FATHER appears.

EVIE

They said she'd been wanting to go to school so badly they couldn't bear to keep her home any longer.

THE FATHER

If she gets to be any trouble to you, though, Ma'am, you send word and we'll take her home again.

EVIE

You won't believe me, Melita, but I felt sorry for the kid. It was rotten luck, getting a bum noggin like that, and I tried to make it work. I really tried. But it kept getting worse … And then that little girl had fourteen fits in one day.

THE GIRL goes into a grand mal seizure, which continues under the following.

EVIE

One. Two. Three. Four. Five. Six. Seven. Eight. Nine. Ten. Eleven. Twelve. Thirteen. Fourteen.

THE GIRL goes limp.

EVIE

I sent word to her father.

*THE FATHER appears and very gently picks THE GIRL up from the
floor and cradles her in his arms.*

THE FATHER

I'm sorry, Miss Bothwell. We're very sorry.

(*to THE GIRL*) Come on, honey. It's time to come home.

They go off.

EVIE

And nobody has seen her since.

Beat.

You know, she used to bring me a bouquet of wildflowers every
morning, and she always came in singing. I never in my life saw
anyone so happy to be at school.

Beat.

They didn't teach us to cope with the fits, Lita. They didn't
teach us to cope with the deaf or the poor or the backward, or
the little genius who finishes all your readers in a year, or the
child who lost half her family to the scarlet fever and doesn't
know why papa cries so much and why isn't mama coming
back. You're supposed to rely on, I don't know, the strength of
your Christian character? Well it's not enough … We are just
two little girls in the woods now, aren't we. So what are we
doing here, Melita? What the hell do we think we're doing
here?

Beat.

Ah, that's Mrs. Nosy-Parker ringing the dinner bell downstairs.
Guess I better go see what's in the trough. Thanks for listening,
anyway. Not like I can talk to anyone here. They still think the
sun shines out of the teacher's patoot—even mine. See ya, Kid.

Your pal—

At that moment, EWART bursts in, breathing hard.

EWART

Miss!

MISS LINTON

Goodness, Ewart, you scared the daylights out of me. Where
were you today?

EWART

Miss, have you heard?

MISS LINTON

Heard what?

EWART

The Gibson kid, over in Baker's Creek. The police came this mornin', they talked to the Souches, they asked me a lotta questions ... I ran here soon as I could get away, but by now the whole county must know.

MISS LINTON

Ewart, what happened to the Gibson child?

EWART

He was attacked. He was beat up pretty bad. They're takin' him to the hospital, they don't know if he's gonna make it.

MISS LINTON

Dear Lord in Heaven. Who did it? Do they know?

EWART

Well, they think they know, alright. That's why I came to tell you ... whatever happens ... I didn't do nothin'.

MISS LINTON

Of course you didn't. Ewart. I guess the police had to ... make enquiries, given your past. But to hurt a little child ... this has nothing to do with you. Everyone with sense will understand that.

EWART looks at her for a beat.

EWART

You just ... I'm awful sorry, Miss. But ... you spend your whole day ... in here, with little kids. You don't know.

MISS LINTON

(*stung*) What don't I know?

EWART

I'm a ... I'm a training school boy, Miss. That's all anyone understands. I just ... whatever happens, I just wanted you to know it wasn't me, I would never do nothin' like that.

MISS LINTON

Well, it would never occur to me to think otherwise.

Beat.

What do you mean, "whatever happens"?

EWART

Folks round here … they're afraid of me, Miss. Even if they can't convict me, they're gonna run me out of town over this, just you wait. They're gonna send me back to …

Beat.

Anyway, anyway. There's nothin' you can do. I'm sorry to bother you. I'm sorry. Good night.

He offers to leave.

MISS LINTON

Wait a minute—Ewart—Do you really—

Beat.

Is that blood on your sleeve?

EWART

I … sorry, Miss, it must be from the hogs. I didn't wash up too good, I guess.

MISS LINTON

What happened to your arm?

EWART

I really gotta—

MISS LINTON

EWART. Stop.

Beat.

Come and let me have a look.

EWART

I thought you said you believed me. That I didn't do nothin'.

MISS LINTON

That's why I need to understand why there's blood on your sleeve. So come here.

EWART

No.

MISS LINTON

Come here and let me have a look.

After several moments of hesitation, EWART complies, rolling up his sleeve and crossing to MISS LINTON. His inner forearm is an ugly mass of old and new knife scars, as far as the elbow—some may be jagged and ridged, or dirty and infected—with fresh cuts still blood-red.

MISS LINTON

    (*in horror and disgust*) Oh ... that's ... just ... awful. Awful. Who did this to you? Ewart, how did you get these horrible cuts on your arm?

EWART

    (*hurriedly rolling his sleeve down and moving off*) I dunno.

MISS LINTON

    Ewart, don't you run away from me again. I forbid you to leave this classroom until you have—

    She puts her hand on his arm—and he flings her across the room.

EWART

    I said NO! You think you can make me? You think you can push me around if I don't let you? Nobody does nothin' to me no more, if I don't let them. You don't understand nothin'. I thought maybe, but ... you just ... You leave me alone, you hear me? You just ... leave me the hell alone!

    He leaves. Slowly, painfully, MISS LINTON picks herself up, and turns to the audience.

END OF ACT I

ACT II

SCENE 1

Jericho School, end of November 1938. THE CHILDREN are in their seats, though EWART is missing, as is RUSSELL.

MISS LINTON
(*to audience*) A week had passed, and still no sign of Ewart. The whole county was abuzz with the uncertain fate of the Gibson child and the police investigation into the attack.

Beat.

However, as Ewart had observed, my job was to spend all day in here with little kids. And education, like time, waited for no one: not for an injured child, or a desperate boy, or his worried teacher. So ...

COLONEL BURNETT
Atten-tion!

COLONEL BURNETT blusters on in full army regalia, complete with impressive white helmet.

MISS LINTON
Class, what do we say to the Inspector of Schools?

THE CHILDREN OF JERICHO
Good morning, Colonel Burnett.

COLONEL BURNETT
Troops! Hands out front!

(*inspecting the proffered fingernails*) Good. Good. Good. Good.

(*he looks around*) Wait a minute. Where in the Sam Hill is your giant?

51

MISS LINTON
Colonel, I would like to talk to you about that—

COLONEL BURNETT
(*waving her away*) Very well, no matter, no matter. Now—
His eyes sweep the frightened assemblage, and alight on the largest remaining object: DWIGHT.
—You. Tall boy.

DWIGHT
(*under his breath*) Oh, no.

COLONEL BURNETT
Up, boy. Up, up, up. To the blackboard, lad—up, up, up, up, I am not in the habit of repeating myself. Now. Which reader?

DWIGHT
Senior Third, sir.

COLONEL BURNETT
Right. Sum of 15,438 and 7,625. Write it down, boy: I doubt your particular genius extends to mental arithmetic. 15,438 and 7,625. Smaller boy!

FLOSSIE
I'm a girl, sir.

COLONEL BURNETT
Hmm. Someone needs to have a word with your mother. Which reader?

FLOSSIE
Senior fourth.

COLONEL BURNETT
Good. 7,623 times 110,462. And don't look to the girl beside you: she's about to have her own troubles.
(*to BERYL*) Whi—

BERYL
(*interrupting*) —Senior Fourth, sir.

COLONEL BURNETT
Interruption! Keenness of mind does not excuse dullness of manners. You will guess what sum I was going to set you, and solve accordingly.
Surveying the trembling little ones who remain, he settles on EFFA.
You, young lady. Which reader?

EFFA
(*standing*) S-s-senior first, s-s-sir.

COLONEL BURNETT
Right. Turn to page fifteen. Reading and comprehension.

EFFA does so—and relaxes into a smile.

COLONEL BURNETT
You know this one? So much the better. Well, out with it, girl, I haven't got all term.

EFFA
(*confidently*) "Three little kittens lost their mittens,
And they began to cry,
'O mother dear, we very much fear
That we have lost our mittens.'
'Lost your mittens!
You naughty kittens—'"

COLONEL BURNETT
—What kind of pie was she going to give them? Eh?—No, don't look. What kind of pie?

Beat.

Too slow, too slow. Sit down. Let's see how our senior scholars are doing.

EFFA sits down, her lower lip starting to wobble. COLONEL BURNETT advances on the older children and their completed sums.

COLONEL BURNETT
(*to DWIGHT*) Wrong.

(*to FLOSSIE*) Wrong.

(*to BERYL, who has done a rather complicated division correctly*) Wrong. That was not the sum I was thinking of, at all. Let that be a lesson to you the next time you want to be insolent with a superior officer

BERYL fights off tears. EFFA, seeing this, cannot contain herself any longer: she plummets to the floor and begins to bawl like a baby. MISS LINTON is about to intervene, but VERN forestalls her.

VERN
It's alright, Teacher. I know what to do.

He gallops over to the desk; retrieves the cod liver oil; and begins advancing on EFFA.

VERN
(*a sing-song warning*) Oh, Effa ...

Sure enough, she clams up at the sight of the dreaded bottle: but he continues forward. At this, BERYL strides over to her sister.

BERYL

(*to VERN*) Don't you dare!

MISS LINTON

That's enough, Vern. Thank you.

VERN shrugs and returns the cod liver oil to its place, as BERYL comforts EFFA. Meanwhile, COLONEL BURNETT is looking around in disbelief.

COLONEL BURNETT

Well … what about me?! Is anyone going to answer my questions?

MILTON

Yes, sir. I am.

They all turn and look at MILTON, who rises from his desk and stares at COLONEL BURNETT with the eyes of a gunslinger.

COLONEL BURNETT

Good, then. Which reader?

MILTON

Second Book, sir.

COLONEL BURNETT

Right you are. Please finish the sum left by the tall boy on the blackboard.

BERYL

But sir, Milton's only—

MILTON

—Twenty-three thousand, sixty-three.

COLONEL BURNETT checks his figures … and looks narrowly back at MILTON.

COLONEL BURNETT

Very well, very well. Recite one verse of your favourite poem, and explain.

MILTON

"What if I say I shall not wait?
What if I—"

He exchanges a look with MISS LINTON.

I mean to say, sir:
"Cannon to right of them,

Cannon to left of them,
Cannon in front of them
Volley'd and thunder'd,
Storm'd at with shot and shell,
Boldly they rode and well,
Into the jaws of Death,
Into the mouth of Hell
Rode the six hundred."

It means, sir … it means they were brave.

COLONEL BURNETT
Very well. What kind of pie was the mother cat going to—

MILTON
—It's a trick, sir. The poem doesn't say what kind of pie.

COLONEL BURNETT
Hmmh. Spell "colonel" for me, boy.

MILTON
Yes, sir. "Colonel": c-o-l-o-n-e-l.

   Beat.

"Bully": b-u-l-l-y.

   The whole class tries desperately to stifle its laughter.

COLONEL BURNETT
(*to the children*) I need to speak to your sergeant. This boy is
clearly in the wrong reader. COMPANY! Fall out!

   They scatter gratefully to the four winds. COLONEL BURNETT
   chuckles ruefully as he removes his helmet and sits with a thump.

COLONEL BURNETT
Good gravyboats. Every year I come here in my best old kit to
scare them stiff so the teacher won't have to. But for all that
young boy cared, I might have been wearing a clown nose and
big pantomime feet.

MISS LINTON
They're good children, Colonel: they really are. I don't think
they need scaring.

COLONEL BURNETT
Not anymore.

   Beat.

Now, according to my records, there are *two* boys missing today.

MISS LINTON

I wanted to speak to you about that, Colonel. Russell Yellowlees has been kept home because some of their calves are colicking—

COLONEL BURNETT

—Well, I'll look into that. And the other boy?

MISS LINTON

Yes, sir, I ... Colonel, have you heard anything about the Gibson case? I mean, do you happen to know, how close are they to ... to ...

COLONEL BURNETT

Miss Linton. You haven't heard, have you?

She shakes her head.

COLONEL BURNETT

It's good news. The child has regained consciousness, and was able to name his assailant. They've arrested a boy from a nearby farm. Not much hope for that lad, I'm afraid ... Training school boy, you know, from Battenville ... name of, what was it again ... Buck Hornsby.

MISS LINTON

Oh, thank goodness. I ... I mean ...

COLONEL BURNETT

I know what you mean. Worried about your own Battenville lad, were you?

MISS LINTON

Yes, Colonel. It's a great relief to know that—that Ewart will not be taken away from us.

COLONEL BURNETT

I wouldn't be too sure of that.

Beat.

The fact is, in the eyes of the community, a scandal like this tars all the boys with the same brush. I can tell you, your trustees are looking to remove the lad, and the Gibson incident is just one of their concerns.

MISS LINTON

I see ...

COLONEL BURNETT

So that's why the boy's not here, is it? Been kept on the farm under lock and key?

56

MISS LINTON
I don't know, sir … Perhaps … But … The truth is, Colonel, I
think Ewart's absence is my fault, actually, and I don't know
what to do about it. I could really use your advice.

COLONEL BURNETT
My advice.

Beat.

Do you know, Miss Linton, despite all my years of teaching
experience, your colleagues see me solely as an annual threat
of unemployment. Not one of them has ever asked me for
advice. Go on, then.

MISS LINTON
Yes, sir. Colonel, suppose a boy chose to confide something to
you, something awful. Suppose you know in your heart that he
needed you to stay calm in the face of that awfulness, but you
… well … let's just say you both handled the situation badly.
And he hasn't been back since.

Beat.

COLONEL BURNETT
Miss Linton, have you considered that this boy is old enough to
know that good people make mistakes?

MISS LINTON
Yes, sir.

COLONEL BURNETT
So what do you teach your children to do when they make a
mistake?

MISS LINTON
Own up to it, and make amends.

Beat.

Oh.

COLONEL BURNETT
Very good. Top of the class. Speaking of which, you'd best
summon your troops so I can sit at the back of your morning
lessons and make a few threatening noises. We must keep up
appearances, after all.

MISS LINTON
Yes, Colonel. Thank you.

SCENE 2

The same day, after school. It is dark. EWART appears in his small, cold room, lit by a lantern. There is a knock at his door.

MISS LINTON

(*offstage*) Ewart? It's Miss Linton.

EWART opens the door. MISS LINTON enters, taking in her surroundings.

MISS LINTON

Right. Thank you for letting me in.

Beat.

Well. This is awkward.

Beat.

Did you hear they arrested someone? For the attack on the Gibson child?

EWART nods.

Oh. Good. It's an open-and-shut case, apparently. It is unfortunate that it was a Battenville boy. But the main thing is, your name is cleared.

Beat.

I do know that's not the only reason you haven't been at school. But I want you to understand something about what happened last week. It was as much my fault as yours.

EWART moves further away.

MISS LINTON

I'm not saying your conduct was acceptable: it was not. The thing is ... I am not very proud of my behaviour, either. When you showed me your arm, I was ... surprised, Ewart. People are sometimes very foolish when ... when they open a drawer and a mouse pops out. They jump.

Beat.

You know, Ewart, I have an uncle who served at Wipers. He has a chest full of medals, and an arm full of shrapnel. Sometimes that arm oozes something awful. I used to change his bandages for him: it was like playing nurse with a real patient! And all the time I was waiting for him to tell me thrilling stories of far-off adventure: but he never did. I was very disappointed. In fact, one day I couldn't stand it any more, so I asked Father:

Why won't Uncle Allan talk about what happened in the War? And he said: Melita … I don't think he has the words.

Beat.

So now we just jaw about anything at all, or sometimes he sits and stares into the distance. Maybe one day he'll have the words. Maybe not.

She reaches into her satchel; pulls out the Junior Red Cross kit; and goes over to the one chair in the room.

MISS LINTON
May I. Please.

Pause. EWART comes and sits on the floor by the chair: he rolls up the same sleeve as before, revealing the welter of cuts and scars. She sits on the chair and begins to clean and dress the wounds. Silence.

EWART
I would never do nothin' to no little kid.

MISS LINTON
I know.

EWART
I didn't mean to do nothin' to you, Miss.

MISS LINTON
Yes, you did.

EWART
I mean, I'm sorry. I'm … sorry.

MISS LINTON
Thank you. I'm sorry, too.

EWART
It don't matter they found who did it. You'll see. One way or another, I'm goin' away. It's only a matter of time.

Beat.

You shouldn't get mixed up in this, Miss. It'll do you no good.

MISS LINTON
Well, thank you, Ewart, for your concern. Other arm, please.

He looks sharply at her, and she meets his gaze impassively. Then he rolls up his other sleeve. That forearm, too, is marked and scarred.

MISS LINTON
Mm-hmm.

She works on the arm.

MISS LINTON

Now, this Gibson business does have everyone on edge. But you belong at Jericho School, Ewart. So I have a plan to keep you there. It has three parts. Part Two: you will go back to class. Part Three: I will talk to all the parents, including the three trustees. I know they want what's best for children, all children: I may just need to remind them of that fact. The trustees' next meeting is after our Christmas concert, where they'll see the whole school—including you—working together, pretty as you please. Then the parents will give the trustees their marching orders, and that will be the end of all this nonsense. Of course, for Parts Two and Three to work, we need Part One. But before I explain what that is, I'm going to ask you to tell me something.

She indicates his arms.

Did someone do this to you?

EWART shakes his head.

MISS LINTON

I see.

Pause.

Uncle Allan is always very gentle with me, but sometimes he does get into scraps. Father explained to me once that, because of where Uncle has been, there are some ... things in his head that build up, like steam in an engine. So once in a while, he just has to let that steam whistle blow. That didn't make sense to me at the time. Does it make sense to you?

EWART nods.

MISS LINTON

Yes. So. Part One.

She takes a bound journal from her satchel and holds it out to him.

MISS LINTON

I want you to promise me, Ewart, that whenever you feel like ... blowing that whistle, you will take to this journal first. Write in it, draw in it, play naughts and crosses, carve it with your jack-knife if you must, but try to put it here ...

Points at the book.

instead of ... anywhere else. Do I have your word that you will try?

60

EWART

Yes, Miss.

MISS LINTON

Good. It goes without saying that I would be honoured if you shared your journal with me someday ... but it is yours now to do with as you please. And that's my plan.

EWART

Miss, I. ... I can't go back to Jericho. You know it and I know it. All this, it won't work, it's no use.

MISS LINTON

Perhaps not: but I do have one more reason why you should try.

She goes to the doorway and calls down the stairs.

You can come up now.

Enter MILTON ... who races right over and throws his arms around EWART.

MILTON

Ewart, you have to come back for the Christmas drill. You're my partner.

MISS LINTON and EWART look at each other.

MISS LINTON

I can expect you then tomorrow for opening exercises?

EWART

Yes, Miss. That's right.

SCENE 3

Jericho Schoolyard. The next morning. The school-bell is ringing. RUSSELL, DWIGHT, and FLOSSIE are loitering outside. EWART comes on. Like the others, he has his books in a leather strap and his lunch in a syrup pail.

RUSSELL

Hey! What're you doin' here?

EWART continues toward the school. RUSSELL blocks him.

RUSSELL

Why don't you go back where you came from, ya criminal.

After a moment, EWART turns around and starts back the way he came.

RUSSELL

Is that what you done to get sent away, too? Beat up on some little kid somewhere? ... Or was it just 'cause your mother's a hooer?

EWART stops and turns back around. He very deliberately puts his book-strap and syrup pail down. RUSSELL takes a fighting stance. EWART responds in kind. Meanwhile, MILTON, EFFA, and VERN pop out of the school. RUSSELL pushes EWART. EWART pushes back. EFFA, sizing up the situation, runs back inside for teacher. MILTON, at imminent risk to life and limb, intercedes.

MILTON

Ewart, Ewart, Ewart, I have a new book for you Ewart, it's very very good, it's by William Butler Yeats, I borrowed it from Mother. Ewart, Ewart, it's inside the school Ewart, come and see, come and see.

Meanwhile, the bell stops. As if waking from a dream, EWART becomes aware of MILTON. With MILTON's help, he picks up his things. MISS LINTON comes racing out with EFFA sidling behind.

MISS LINTON

What's going on out here? Is everything alright?

RUSSELL

Nothin' going on here, Teacher. Nothin' at all.

MISS LINTON

Well, then, get inside, all of you. We're ready to begin.

They all troop inside, MILTON prattling away beside EWART.

MILTON

Wait'll you read this book, Ewart. It has some very, very good ones, like listen to this:

"Come away, O human child!
To the waters and the wild
With a faery, hand in hand,
For the world's more full of weeping than you can understand ... "

SCENE 4

All around the Jericho School community, December 1938. In the local church, MRS. BAPTIE addresses the members of the choir.

MRS. BAPTIE

Good afternoon, choir. Thank you for coming to practice on such a blustery snowy day. Let's get our hymn-books ready at page one hundred and fifty-three, shall we?

She comes over to MISS LINTON, who has been surreptitiously checking the door.

MRS. BAPTIE

Don't worry: he'll be here.

MISS LINTON

I'm sorry, Mrs. Baptie?

MRS. BAPTIE

Clinton Cochrane.

MISS LINTON

Well ... thank you, Mrs. Baptie, but I am not really interested in the comings and goings of Mr. Cochrane.

MRS. BAPTIE

Oh, that's not what Effa tells us. She says you blush up like a beetroot if he even drives down the road. Take your time, you two: but for the rest of us, it's like trying to read a story when we already know the ending!

MISS LINTON

Mrs. Baptie—

MRS. BAPTIE

Now, now: I approve entirely. It's good to take an interest in local affairs—so to speak. Why, before you came, Beryl and Effa had a "suitcase teacher." Not a real teacher at all. Went home to her own people every weekend, if you please, as if she couldn't be bothered with us. Didn't go to church here or run a jumble sale ... Didn't even play euchre! ... Anyway. We're so glad Beryl has you as an example.

Beat.

I hope my girls don't give you any trouble.

MISS LINTON

Heavens, no, Mrs. Baptie—

MRS. BAPTIE

—Good, because with that training school boy in your classroom, you have enough to worry about. Especially when he's a suspect for *attempted murder.*

MISS LINTON

Oh, now, Mrs. Baptie, the Gibson boy's attacker has been caught, and it had nothing to do with Ewart Rokosh. So I don't think anyone needs to worry about Ewart. I think he's fine where he is.

MRS. BAPTIE

But Miss Linton. Effa told me he has knife-scars on his arms. All over his arms, like a knife-fighter. She saw it one day when he rolled up his sleeves to split the firewood.

Beat.

MISS LINTON

Mrs. Baptie, Ewart has had some troubles in the past, but—

MRS. BAPTIE

—Effa says he went off on the bigger children for the sake of a little Hallowe'en prank. Nearly put them in the hospital. He even threatened you with a snake, for goodness' sake. That boy is not right in the head, Miss Linton. He shouldn't be around normal children. That's what my husband is going to say at the trustees' meeting.

MISS LINTON

But ... but ...

CLINTON COCHRANE enters the church.

CLINTON

Good morning, Miss Linton ... Oh, hello, Mrs. Baptie. I'm sorry, I didn't see you there.

MRS. BAPTIE

(*twinkling*) I'm sure you didn't, Clinton. Never mind. Pay no attention to me. I'm not even here.

MRS. BAPTIE moves off.

CLINTON

Miss Linton?

MISS LINTON

(*snapping*) What is it, Mr. Cochrane.

CLINTON

I—Uh ... never mind.

MRS. BAPTIE

Thank you, everyone. Would you all please look at page one hundred and fifty-three: "Children of the Heavenly Father."

THE CHOIR
> "Children of the heav'nly Father
> Safely in His bosom gather;
> Nestling bird nor star in Heaven
> Such a refuge e'er was given ... "

EWART appears, reading from his journal.

EWART

One time in music class, Mr. Lebeau was telling us how his battalion liberated this village in France, and the people made them a big feast of ortolans. He said ortolans are little baby songbirds that get captured and they have food forced down their throats all day for two or three weeks until they fatten up to twice or thrice the size they should be. Then they drown the birds in a bucket of brandy; pluck them; and put them in the oven, with the head and guts and all. When they bring them to the table, you have to be ready. You have to drink as much brandy as you can stand; put a napkin over your head, so you get all the smell of the bird; and plunk the whole bird in your mouth.

In MILTON's family home, MISS LINTON and the COYTES have just finished supper. MR. COYTE is drinking.

MISS LINTON

Well, thank you, Mrs. Coyte. Dinner was delicious, as always. And thank you for loaning me that Bliss Carman collection. You have a very fine library.

MRS. COYTE

Oh, don't mention it, Miss Linton. Mr. Coyte and I have always enjoyed having Milton's teachers over for dinner—but in your case, it is a particular pleasure.

MR. COYTE

Mmmh.

MRS. COYTE

It's not often that we get such stimulating company. And Milton is obviously in good hands at your school.

MISS LINTON

I shall take that as a compliment, Mrs. Coyte—coming, as it does, from a fellow teacher.

MRS. COYTE

Oh, you know, my teaching days are long over, dear. Ever since I met Ewan.

MR. COYTE
Mmmh.

MRS. COYTE
You know how it is: no married lady teachers, and so forth, and I don't expect that will ever change.

MISS LINTON
No, I don't expect that it will.

MRS. COYTE
Nor should it. After all, you can't serve two masters.

Beat.

Well, I'd better go help Milton with the washing-up.

MISS LINTON
I'll help, too.

MRS. COYTE
No, no, dear—you're the teacher.

She leaves. MISS LINTON smiles at MR. COYTE. Slight pause.

MR. COYTE
It's a good name. Ewart. Good name.

MISS LINTON
Oh. Yes. Yes, it's a fine name.

MR. COYTE
Ewart—Rokosh.

MISS LINTON
Yes. I believe it's Polish.

MR. COYTE
Hmh. Catholic.

Beat.

MISS LINTON
Milton is quite devoted to him.

MR. COYTE
Makes a change from being led around by women.

Beat.

What was the boy sent away for? Gangs?

MISS LINTON
I don't know, Mr. Coyte, but—

MR. COYTE
—Miss Linton, you're a good teacher. But some things come into a community that don't ever belong there. Milton won't

say anything against him, but we heard from Zellah Baptie that
he hit a girl. And broke Russell Yellowlees' jaw, pretty near.

MISS LINTON

Yes, defending your son. And I'm sure he could have broken it
clean through if he'd wanted to.

(*recovering herself*) What I mean to say is …

Beat.

Mr. Coyte, I wish I could tell you that Milton will eventually fit
in. He won't. Milton stands out. He's a wonderful, loving,
intelligent boy, and I wouldn't change him for all the tea in
China. But right now he needs a protector and a pal—a big
brother, in fact—and he's found one in Ewart.

MR. COYTE

That's what I'm afraid of.

MRS. COYTE enters.

MISS LINTON

Sir, you needn't be. Ewart is not a thug. Milton is lucky to have
a friend who shares his love of language, of poetry, but also
someone who can teach him to take care of himself. At the
same time, Milton is teaching Ewart how to take care of
another human being. That's exactly how it's supposed to be.

Beat.

We all know that Ewart has strayed in the past, but hasn't every
one of us, at one time or another, needed someone to give us a
second chance? The welcoming of the prodigal son … is that
not, in fact, our Christian duty?

Beat.

MR. COYTE

Anyone ever learn to say "no" to you?

MISS LINTON

(*smiling*) Not yet.

(*to MRS. COYTE*) You see my point, too, don't you, Mrs. Coyte?
As a fellow teacher?

Beat.

MRS. COYTE

That boy is trouble, Miss Linton. I know everyone in this
community, but I don't know the first thing about the kind of
people he comes from—except that they couldn't manage him.

So then how can *we*? That's what trained professionals are for: doctors and nurses—and guards—and so forth. You just teach our children, Miss Linton. You're good at it.

(*as she starts off*) Mr. Coyte and I can't *wait* to see what you're going to do with the Christmas concert.

MR. COYTE
Mmmh.

MRS. COYTE
… Now I wonder if you would have a look at Milton's costume for the skit?

EWART reads from his journal.

EWART
You don't put the head in your mouth, though. The ortolan's head you let hang out your lips like the cat that caught the canary. Then you crunch it up, bones and all, and the bird's lungs are drowned full of brandy so they pop in your mouth like cherries. The brandy and the grease and the sauce run all out of your mouth and down your chin. Then you nip off the head, and swallow. The villagers told Mr. Lebeau it's the most wonderful taste in the whole wide world.

Beat.

I don't think Mr. Lebeau should have liberated France. I think he should have let it be.

A bell rings at the local euchre night as three players sit at the table: MR. and MRS. VARNUM (DWIGHT's parents), and MISS LINTON.

MR. VARNUM
(*he speaks genially and deliberately*) Well, it's awf'lly nice to see you at one of our church euchres, Miss Linton. Is this your first tournament?

MISS LINTON
Thank you, Mr. Varnum, yes: I have been studying the rules, and I thought it was high time I gave it a try.

Beat.

While we're waiting, I wondered if I could talk to you both about one of the boys at our school. You see—

MRS. NEEDLER (FLOSSIE's mother) storms in.

MR. VARNUM
You're slow, Millie.

MRS. NEEDLER
> My table was slow. The Hoopers think this is a chin-wagging tournament. And Howard Souch wouldn't know a low bower if it socked him in the nose. It's not fair. How am I ever s'pposed to win this thing when they keep partnering me with fools?
>
> *She begins to deal.*

MR. VARNUM
> Well, buck up, Millie: you've got Miss Linton now.
>
> (*to MISS LINTON*) It's awf'lly nice to have you. My wife and I are sure glad you straightened out our little Dwight, aren't we, Mother?
>
> *MRS. VARNUM nods.*

MR. VARNUM
> I told him not to give you no more trouble or he'll get it twice as bad at home. From me, and then from his big brothers. Isn't that right, Mother?
>
> *MRS. VARNUM nods.*

MR. VARNUM
> Anyway, it's awf'lly nice to have you—

MRS. NEEDLER
> —You've said that already, Lionel.

MR. VARNUM
> Alright, then, Millie.
>
> (*turning back to MISS LINTON*) Oh, just so's you know—we always call out the cards for Mother's sake. My lady wife's eyesight is not too good with the cataracts, is it, Mother?
>
> *MRS. VARNUM is holding the cards about two inches from her nose. She shakes her head.*

MISS LINTON
> Well, certainly: that's no trouble, Mrs. Varnum.
>
> *They pick up their cards—except MRS. NEEDLER, who turns a card up from the deck.*

MRS. NEEDLER
> Alright: let's get a move on. The turn card's King of spades.
>
> *MR. VARNUM addresses MRS. NEEDLER, just as she is about to pick up her own cards.*

MR. VARNUM

  Say, Millie: is that girl of yours still scrappin' up a storm with
  the boys? Dwight says you should give Flossie a pair of gloves
  and send her off for to beat Joe Louis. Pass.

  MRS. NEEDLER flares up.

MISS LINTON

  Oh, now, Mr. Varnum—pass—that's not really—

MRS. NEEDLER

  —I don't know what gives you the right to judge, Lionel—

MRS. VARNUM

  Pass.

MRS. NEEDLER

  —But at least my girls only taught Flossie to take care of
  herself. I guess your boys taught Dwight to steal cows' heads
  from the—

MR. VARNUM

  (*mildly*)—Your turn, Millie. Better get a move on.

MRS. NEEDLER

  Fine. I take it up.

  (*she takes the card*) Your boys taught Dwight to—

MR. VARNUM

  —Aren't you going to check your hand first?

MRS. NEEDLER

  See, this is how a table gets behind, Lionel. Time gets wasted by
  people that don't know what they're doin'. If you three passed
  on it, any idiot can tell that—

  She glances at her cards and stops dead.

MR. VARNUM

  (*enjoying himself immensely*) Can tell that what, Millie?

MRS. NEEDLER

  Nothing. Nothing.

  (*she discards*) Come on, Lionel. Quit stallin'.

MR. VARNUM

  Okay then. Ace of hearts.

MISS LINTON

  Uh ... ten of diamonds.

MRS. VARNUM

  Jack of hearts.

MRS. NEEDLER
King of hearts. Take it, Lionel.

MR. VARNUM
Alright, then. Queen of hearts.

Beat.

Miss Linton?

MISS LINTON
(*staring at her cards*) Oh, fiddlesticks. Alright, then. Ten of spades.

MRS. NEEDLER
You WHAT?

MISS LINTON
(*more tentatively*) Ten of spades?

MRS. NEEDLER glowers.

MRS. VARNUM
Ace of spades. Sorry, Millie.

MRS. NEEDLER growls and buries herself in her cards.

MR. VARNUM
(*amiably*) Something wrong, Millie? You're holdin' us up, you know.

MRS. NEEDLER
(*slamming it down*) Jack of clubs takes it.

MR. VARNUM
There, see? I knew you'd prevail.

MRS. NEEDLER
Don't be an ass. King of spades.

MR. VARNUM
Ten of clubs.

MISS LINTON
Oh. Uh ... the ... no, the Queen of clubs. I was wondering, actually, if I could talk to you all about, uh ...

MRS. VARNUM
Jack of spades takes it. King of diamonds.

MRS. NEEDLER
King of clubs.

MISS LINTON
... about the upcoming trustees' meeting?

MR. VARNUM

Oh, I wouldn't worry about that, Miss Linton. I'm sure your Christmas concert will be excellent. Nine of diamonds.

MISS LINTON

Thank you, Mr. Varnum—but it's not my job I'm worried about. It's—

MR. VARNUM

—And none of us are trustees, as you know.

MISS LINTON

Yes, I know, but I was hoping you might—

MRS. NEEDLER

—Miss Linton.

MISS LINTON

What? Oh dear, I'm so sorry. I—

(*looks at cards*) Oh. OH. Well, I just happen to have the—ACE—of diamonds! We win the trick, Mrs. Needler!

MRS. NEEDLER

(*staring at her*) Son of a—

MR. VARNUM

—Please, Mrs. Needler. There are ladies present.

MRS. NEEDLER

You tossed the Queen of clubs.

MISS LINTON

Oh, did I? I guess … but … we won the trick! Jack of diamonds, Mrs. Varnum.

MRS. VARNUM

Queen of diamonds. Sorry, Millie.

MRS. NEEDLER

Son of a bitch. Ace of clubs.

MR. VARNUM

Ten of hearts. You're euchred, Millie.

MRS. NEEDLER

I KNOW THAT.

A bell rings. MRS. NEEDLER rises and turns the full bore of her rage upon MISS LINTON.

MISS LINTON

I'm sorry, Mrs. Needler. I—

72

MRS. NEEDLER

 —Some are born fools; some achieve foolishness ... and some have fools thrust upon 'em.

 She storms off.

MISS LINTON

 Oh dear. Oh dear.

MR. VARNUM

 Now, Miss Linton, don't you worry about the Widow Needler. We've watched her stompin' and flouncin' about ever since we all started at Jericho School: haven't we, Mother?

 MRS. VARNUM nods. The VARNUMS rise from the table.

MR. VARNUM

 Well, better get to our next round.

MISS LINTON

 (*very upset*) ... But ... but I was going to ask you all to put in a good word for Ewart Rokosh ... before the trustees' meeting. Oh, dear.

MR. VARNUM

 Oh, now, don't you worry, don't you worry, Miss Linton. Mother's going to get you a glass of water.

 (... *and MRS. VARNUM has indeed shuffled purposefully off*)

 Now, look: we all know how hard you been pullin' for that Battenville boy. And myself, I've been thinkin' maybe I haven't given the boy a fair shake. You believe in him, and that oughtta be good enough for me.

MISS LINTON

 Thank you, but I don't think it was good enough for Mrs. Needler.

MR. VARNUM

 Oh, don't worry about Millie. The trustees are all you need to keep him in school.

 (*MRS. VARNUM returns with the water*)

 Now, the Bapties are dead set against the boy, of course—but Coyte's on the fence now, 'tween you and his wife: and 'tween you and his wife I know which side I'd rather come down on ... No, the one you need to get to is Callum Yellowlees. I'll have a word with him, if you like. He's awful grateful for what you done with Vern this past while. He just might give it a think.

MISS LINTON
Thank you.

EWART reads from his journal.

EWART
... I think being a child is like you're going around with a tiny bird in your hand, and at some point they take this bird and gently crush it, so you can just barely hear the little bones crack. Then they hand it back to you, and you carry it with you for the rest of your life. Yes, that's childhood.

SCENE 5

Jericho School classroom. Middle of December.

The children, in various stages of costuming, run through the place like a tornado, and in the twinkling of an eye, a Christmas tree appears, and the Christmas concert stage is set up—with its iconic curtain of bedsheets mounted on wires, behind which the children promptly disappear. Well, "disappear" is perhaps a misleading term, since throughout the following, the curtain ripples with bodies poking and peeking and bumping, and the occasional "Hi, Mum!" is heard from between the curtains. Meanwhile, MRS. BAPTIE bears down on MISS LINTON with a biscuit-tin cash box.

MRS. BAPTIE
Miss Linton! Miss Linton! The Christmas concert is a success!

MISS LINTON
But it hasn't started yet, Mrs. Baptie.

MRS. BAPTIE
Oh, I know, Miss Linton, and I'm sure it will be grand. But we've already raised even more than last year: that'll buy some new books for the bookshelf, and maybe even a map of Great Britain! I think everyone in the township is here! Good afternoon, Miss Bothwell ...

EVIE comes in.

MISS LINTON
Evie!

They embrace.

What are you doing here?

74

EVIE

Are you kidding? I wouldn't miss your concert: it'll be better than the picture-show! Besides, I miss you, kid. See me after class.

She goes off to take her seat.

MRS. BAPTIE

... And here's another of your fellow teachers.

CLINTON COCHRANE enters.

MISS LINTON

Oh, no, Mrs. Baptie. Mr. Cochrane's not a teacher.

MRS. BAPTIE

Hah! Shows what you know. I'll just leave you two alone ...

She sails off, humming. MISS LINTON looks inquiringly at CLINTON.

CLINTON

Well, I did teach at Bonner's School, but that was a quite a while ago.

MISS LINTON

You surprise me, Mr. Cochrane. What made you give it up?

CLINTON

Oh, I just did it long enough to get the money for university. I mean, it's not like it's a real job—

MISS LINTON

—Oh, really—

CLINTON

(*hurriedly*)—For a man. I was going to say, "for a man." A little country school is honourable work and all of that: but you have to admit, the way these old tightwads pay you, it's not a career.

MISS LINTON

Indeed.

CLINTON

No, it's not. That's why we men go back to school, and you women get married. There's no future in this, and I needed to have a future in case ... in case I ever met a wonderful girl.

MISS LINTON

Well, best of luck with that, Mr. Cochrane. And if ever you do meet one—that wants you—be sure to send me a telegram.

CLINTON slinks off toward his seat.

MISS LINTON
(*to the audience*) We started with the drill, which went off as well
as could be expected. Then came skits, songs, recitations;
Russell and Dwight on the mouth organ; and finally, the big
skit, which I had written specially for the occasion.
> *MILTON comes on in businessman's attire, with a cardboard*
> *briefcase. He is now "acting in a skit."*

MILTON
Gee, it sure is good to be a banker from the city.
> *Hisses and boos from behind the curtain.*

MILTON
Everyone would really be a lot better off if they thought just
what I thought, and did just what I do.
> *BERYL, DWIGHT, and VERN come on, as farmers.*

BERYL
Please, Mr. Banker, be nice to us.

VERN
Our crops didn't grow this year.

DWIGHT
We don't want to lose our farm.

MILTON
No. Go away. What do you want a dirty old farm for, anyway?
You are just asking for trouble.
> *Sings a patter-song accompanied by MISS LINTON on piano, and*
> *clearly aspiring to be by Noel Coward.*

Everyone
Should be like me.
It is the only possible way to be.
You country hicks from in the sticks don't know where your
bread is buttered;
If we thought like you, we'd be in a stew, and the shops would
all be shuttered!
Everyone
Should be like me!
> *BERYL, DWIGHT, and VERN exit as FLOSSIE, RUSSELL, and*
> *EWART come on, dressed as a Ukrainian, a French-Canadian,*
> *and an "Indian," respectively.*

MILTON
Now what do you want?

76

FLOSSIE

Please, sir.

EWART

Our children are hungry, and we have no homes to go to.

RUSSELL

We want … we want the …

EWART

(*prompting him*) "We want you please to show some Christian charity and help us get on our feet in this great land."

RUSSELL

We want you please to … we want your help.

MILTON

Oh, really? Then why don't you give up your funny ways and your funny ideas and become just like me? I'll help you. Let's start with that silly hat.

He grabs for RUSSELL's hat, and they pantomime a struggle.

RUSSELL

Hey mister, you can't take my hat. My mother made me this ha—ow!!! You little—

In getting the hat away from him, MILTON has managed to whack RUSSELL in the nose again. RUSSELL, furious, is about to go for him, but is firmly ushered off by EWART as MISS LINTON hurriedly plays the introduction to the next verse. FLOSSIE reacts to being left alone on stage with MILTON.

MILTON

Everyone
Should be like me.
It is the only possible way to be.
My trust you must earn, I've nothing to learn, and I find it rather queer,
If you know so much, with your ways and such, then what are you doing here?
Everyone
Should be like me!

Exit FLOSSIE. Above the curtain appears EFFA, dressed like an angel.

MILTON

Oh my stars, it's an angel! Hello, beautiful angel. I am so glad to see you!

EFFA

I don't think so.

MILTON

What makes you say that?

EFFA

Because you only care for people who are just like you. But you do not have beautiful wings, and I do. Say, why don't you come and pull off my wings? Then I'll be just like you, and you will like me.

MILTON

Well … alright. I guess that makes sense.

He goes toward her.

EFFA

WAIT! Mortal man, you cannot sing like me either—hymns of praise that gladden all who hear them.

Sings "O Holy Night."

"Fall on your knees! O hear the angel voices!"

(*she stops*) But that's not like you either, so I shall never sing again.

MILTON

Oh, no, angel. It would be terrible not to use that beautiful voice, just because it's not like me. I guess there is more than one way to be a good person, after all.

The children all join in the (slightly truncated) carol:

THE CHILDREN OF JERICHO

"Fall on your knees! O hear the angel voices!"

They skip to the high part.

"O night divine!
O night, O night divine!"

They bow, and EWART closes the curtain. MISS LINTON stands up from the piano.

MISS LINTON

(*to the audience*) Then came the nativity play, which was the same as all nativity plays since the Nativity itself. Then it was Santa Claus. Now, the only person who could be persuaded to don the costume that year was Mr. Coyte.

MR. COYTE appears, swaying, as Santa.

MR. COYTE
(*darkly*) Ho. Ho. Ho.

> *He sits with a thump. CLINTON appears at MISS LINTON's side.*

CLINTON
I know you don't want to see me, Miss Linton, but I just wanted to warn you: Farmer Claus over there is about seven sheets to the wind.

> *VERN toddles up to MR. COYTE—who looks at the child; consults his list; looks at the child again; and addresses him solemnly.*

MR. COYTE
... And who the hell are you?

MISS LINTON
Oh, dear ...

> *In a flash, CLINTON is escorting the wobbling 'Santa' toward the exit.*

CLINTON
Ho, ho, ho, right this way, Mr. Claus. Ho, ho, ho.

MR. COYTE
Wait, wait. I'm sure there's a few more of the little basta—

CLINTON
—Ho, ho, ho, kids. Santa just needs to ... to feed his reindeer. He'll be right back.

MISS LINTON
(*brightly*) In the meantime, let us all sing, "Deck the Halls."

> *She bangs it out on the piano as everyone joins in.*

ALL
"Deck the halls with boughs of holly,
Fa la la la la, la la la la.
'Tis the season to be jolly,
Fa la la la la, la la la la.
Don we now our gay apparel,
Fa la la, la la la, la la la.
Troll the ancient Yule tide carol,
Fa la la la la, la la la la."

> *During this, there is much scuffling outside ... and CLINTON comes back in wearing the Santa outfit—slightly askew.*

CLINTON

Ho, ho, ho, that's better: a little fresh air, and Santa feels like a new man! Say, who's the next good little child to get their present?

MISS LINTON

I am very glad to have you here. Santa Claus.

She shares a look with CLINTON.

Go ahead, children.

CLINTON welcomes VERN at one end of the room, and the other children gather round, playing and chattering. MR. YELLOWLEES enters on the other side. MISS LINTON makes a beeline for him.

MISS LINTON

Mr. Yellowlees! Sir, I was wondering if I could speak to you for a minute.

MR. YELLOWLEES

Okay.

MISS LINTON

Good. First of all, I hope you enjoyed the concert—

MR. YELLOWLEES

—Yes I did, Miss Linton. Fact I'd say that was pretty near the best concert I ever seen at Jericho. You're a good teacher.

MISS LINTON

Oh, it's easy when the children work so well together. Sir, I know those boys have had their differences, but I was hoping, at your trustees' meeting—

MR. YELLOWLEES

—Miss Linton, we had our meeting last week.

Beat.

Now, we all respect what you done for Jericho, and we kept the Rokosh boy on so's not to spoil your concert. The thing is, he can't stay here.

MISS LINTON

But Mr. Yellowlees—he hasn't done anything …

MR. YELLOWLEES

(*beat*) These are your students, Miss Linton: but they're our *children*. Now, if a convicted felon moved next door to your family—got in fights with your boy—and one of his prison chums beat a child near to death, just down the road: are you telling me you wouldn't do exactly what we done?

Beat.

Thought so. Tomorrow, that boy goes back to Battenville School.

He moves off—as MISS LINTON catches sight of EWART, who has been listening the whole time. He runs off.

MISS LINTON
Ewart!

CLINTON
Ho, ho, ho!

SCENE 6

Jericho Schoolyard (continuous). EWART runs on with his coat and bookstrap in his arms and throws them on the ground. He is hurriedly taking off his nativity costume when MISS LINTON appears.

EWART
Miss ... Please, Miss—please—you have to let me go.

MISS LINTON
Go where, Ewart?

EWART
Away.

MISS LINTON
Away where, exactly? To live on the streets? End your days in some hobo camp? It's a hard world out there, Ewart. You don't want to face it on your own.

EWART
I am on my own. My step-mum's all that's left, and she won't even see me since I got took. And here, I'm just "the training school boy." That's why I need to go.

MISS LINTON
You have another choice. You can go back to Battenville.

EWART
Miss Linton. I will die before I go back there.

MISS LINTON
Why? Why was it such a terrible place?

EWART

I will die.

MISS LINTON

I see.

Beat.

Ewart ... what did you do? To get sent to Battenville.

Beat.

EWART

I'm ... I'm a thief, Miss. When Pop died, my step-mum didn't want to pay for my keep, so she sent me out to steal it. Till I got caught.

Beat.

Miss ... I'm awful grateful you tried to help me. But it's more than your job's worth, and ... I'm not worth that. You're a good teacher.

MISS LINTON

Yes, I am.

Beat.

Alright, Ewart: go.

EWART

What?

MISS LINTON

There's never going to be a better time than now. Paper! Pencil!

She snatches up one of EWART's notebooks; he hands her a pencil; and she begins to write furiously.

MISS LINTON

Do you know the Hoopers' place, where I'm boarding?

EWART

Yes, Miss.

MISS LINTON

Good. Go up to the little attic room. Under the bed, there's a small trunk where you'll find twenty dollars. Take ten dollars and get yourself to the six o'clock train.

EWART

Miss, I can't—

MISS LINTON

Don't worry. The entire township is here, including the
Hoopers. Now, this is a letter to my cousin Cora in Souris,
Manitoba. They're farming three sections there. That's a lot.

EWART

Miss, I—

MISS LINTON

—Cora's an ex-teacher. She'll help you get into high school.
You will get your education, young man, and do me proud.
And if you throw away this chance and end up dead in a hobo
camp, I swear I'll come and find your corpse and wring its
bloody neck.

EWART

Miss, I can't ... I can't steal your money and run away.

MISS LINTON

Nonsense, Ewart, it's not stealing if I give it to you.

EWART

They could run you out of town over this. They could make
you stop teachin'.

MISS LINTON

Oh, I don't have to bother about teaching. Apparently, it's not
a real job, and anyway, I'm going to marry Clinton Cochrane.
Or so I'm told.

EWART

Miss ... why are you doin' this for me?

MISS LINTON

(*simply*) ... Because I care about you.

    CLINTON enters.

CLINTON

(*to MISS LINTON*) Is everything alright out here? The children
sent me to find you. Clearly, they'd rather have you than Santa.

(*sees EWART, with concern*) Son, are you alri—

MISS LINTON

—Mr. Cochrane—I need you to do something for me, *right
now*.

CLINTON

What is it?

MISS LINTON
> Drive Ewart to the Hoopers' place. Let him get ten dollars
> from the trunk in my room. Then take him to the train station.
> And don't discuss it with anyone.

CLINTON
> But why—

MISS LINTON
> —*Clinton.* I'll explain everything, I promise you—but right now,
> I need your help. Just get this boy to the six o'clock train.
> Please.

CLINTON
> (*beat*) Of course.
>
> (*to EWART*) I'll get the truck warmed up. Meet me there in
> about a minute.
>
> *CLINTON leaves. Pause.*

MISS LINTON
> Hurry, Ewart. We haven't much time.

EWART
> (*with great difficulty*) Yes, Miss ... This is—
>
> *He hands her the book of poetry.*
>
> —for Milton. And—
>
> *He cannot continue.*

MISS LINTON
> Now, if you get me crying before I have to go back in there, I
> will never forgive you. Run along, Ewart, before I come to my
> senses. Just one more thing: write me at Hoopers', to let me
> know how you're getting on. Under the name of Dickinson.
>
> *EWART awkwardly holds out his journal to her.*

MISS LINTON
> Oh, Ewart, I can't take that. You have to keep writing.

EWART
> I will, Miss. I always will. But this is for you.
>
> *She takes the journal, and he leaves. After a moment, EVIE pops
> out.*

EVIE
> Well, now the kids are missing you AND Santa Claus. Better
> come inside, Lita. People will talk.

MISS LINTON

Yes, Evie: I expect they will ... You go on. I'll be right in.

EVIE disappears. MISS LINTON opens EWART's journal, and reads.

MISS LINTON

"What if I say I shall not wait?
What if I burst the fleshly gate
And pass, escaped, to thee?
What if I file this mortal off,
See where it hurt me,—that's enough,—
And wade in liberty?

They cannot take me any more,—"

EWART appears, as before, reading from his journal.

EWART

(*overlapping*) "They cannot take me any more,—
Dungeons may call, and guns implore;
Unmeaning now, to me,
As laughter was an hour ago,
Or laces, or a travelling show,
—Or who died yesterday!"

Beat.

My whole life, people have been trying to make me into
nothing. It would be so easy to finish the job. Anyway, no
matter what I do, it'll always be there: the nothingness. Miss
Linton, you asked me once what the poem means. Maybe one
day you'll read this and you'll have your answer.

Beat.

You know, the day you gave me this journal, you saved my life.
The crazy thing is, my life seems to mean something to you,
like I hope someday it'll mean something to me. That's a
miracle, Miss. I think that's my miracle.

... And he is gone.

MISS LINTON

(*she closes the journal*) Well.

(*to the audience*) This is what I wanted to tell you. All my young
life, I thought I knew what it meant to be a teacher. But when I
said good-bye to Ewart ... that's when I understood.

*As she speaks, she transforms back into the elderly woman from the
beginning of the play.*

Oh, that's quite enough about me, anyway.

Beat.

S.S. #1, Jericho School.

Beat.

Outside: four strong walls. Not strong enough, in the end, to stay the wrecking ball of change. Inside: one room. Built to hold everyone this place ever grew: yet always too small. Always someone somehow got left in the cold. —A wood stove. Warm, familiar, cranky, dangerous. —Blackboards: could have opened the whole world to children, if only I'd known something of the world at the time.

Beat.

But we did have one perfect thing, perched on the top of this flawed kingdom: a bell. Our bell called children through shining fields on cold mornings. And this is what it said:

There is a place for you in this world.
There is a place for you in this world.
Come in. Sit down. Sit up straight! Let us begin.

… And the school bell rings out.

THE END

GLOSSARY

Normal School: Teacher's College. At the time of this story, a one-year certification programme could be taken directly after high school.

Big Boys: Teenage boys who were kept back in elementary school, usually because they had to stay home for much of the year to help with running the farm. They were often the bane of a country schoolteacher's existence.

Wipers: Soldiers' slang for Ypres, site of major battles fought by Canadians in World War I. The Second Battle of Ypres marked the first wartime use of chlorine gas. Vimy Ridge, where Boyd Lebeau fought, was another fearsome battle in which Canadians were heavily involved. Col. Burnett, meanwhile, may well have been involved in the Boer War as well as WWI.

Readers: While a child might have other schoolbooks, the mainstay of elementary education was the reader. Distributed by the province, these four books of literary and historical excerpts were the core curriculum of primary school, and also determined what grade a student was in. So, "Junior First" was what we would call Grade One; "Senior First" was equivalent to Grade Two, "Junior Second" was like Grade Three, and so on. (There was also an introductory book called a primer which roughly corresponded to kindergarten). However, the teacher could decide when it was appropriate to advance a child to the next reader in the middle of the year, or to hold her back at the end of it. Or children could be at different levels in different subjects. In other words, the system was as about as flexible as its teacher.

Entrance exams: At this time, entrance to high school was only gained by passing a standardised test at the end of the Senior Fourth

(Grade Eight) year. This was a terrifying prospect to many, and some children never made it over the hurdle.

Training schools: Residential reform schools for juvenile delinquents (with separate institutions for boys and for girls). Found throughout Ontario in the first three-quarters of the twentieth century (and similar to institutions found across North America), they were meant to offer education, vocational training, structure, and stability to wayward youth who had been committed by the police, the courts, or their parents. Children as young as eight years old were sent to the schools, and length of stay was indefinite, though most residents were in their early teens and remained for about eighteen months. Bowmanville Training School for Boys was particularly known for its agricultural programme, and for sending about forty percent of its boys out to work on farms in the region after their term at the school was finished.

I have been told that many dedicated teachers and counsellors worked at these centres, and that many troubled boys and girls were put on the straight and narrow and went on to have happy and productive lives. However, there were also children who did not fare so well. It seems that sadists and sexual predators found their way into these institutions—as is inevitable, I think, whenever vulnerable children are gathered together and separated from people who love them. In the 1990s, lawsuits began which alleged massive amounts of sexual, physical, and emotional abuse at training schools across the province, dating back decades. For information on these lawsuits, I spoke to Loretta Merritt of the law firm Torkin Manes.

Souch: English surname, pronounced "such."

Catlow: Irish name, pronounced "cat´-loe."

Anti-I-Over: Pronounced "an´-tee-eye-oe´-ver": a variant of tag. Team X tosses ball over top of shed or outhouse to Team Y. Whoever gets the ball has to go, with the rest of Team Y, to the Team X side of the building and tag as many Team X players as she can. (Her teammates try to help by herding, blocking, and misdirecting the X team to prevent them from escaping to the other side of the building.) Anyone she tags has to switch to her team. This goes on until all players are on the same team—or until the bell rings, which is far more likely. The game had many names—Annie-Annie-Over, Andrew-Over—but was played in almost identical fashion across rural North America for decades, until disappearing entirely in the latter part of the twentieth century (probably with the disappearance of school outhouses and woodsheds.) It usually involved a soft, spongy ball, for reasons of safety, but I have imagined that Russell, boss of the schoolyard, would think that soft balls were for sissies.

Gene Stratton-Porter: American author of *Freckles* and *Girl of the Limberlost*. The JK Rowling of her day.

Water belly: Urinary calculi (that is, painful stones in the urinary tract) in sheep, goats, and cattle. Rare in females.

Euchre: A card game, and a staple of rural life. Here is a summary of the game played by Miss Linton, and written with the help of Jonathan Sy:

Initial hands:

West (Mr. Varnum): AQ10h, 10c, 9d
North (Miss Linton): AJ10d, Qc, 10s
East (Mrs. Varnum): KQd, AJs, Jh
South, the dealer (Mrs. Needler): K9h, AKJc

Ks is the turn card.

1) West passes.
2) North passes.
3) East passes.
4) a) South, in the midst of a quarrel, takes the King without looking at her hand.
   b) She realises that she has a terrible hand, but knows that odds are good that she can make it anyway: she's relying on her partner for one trick, and the game is secure.
   c) South discards the 9 of hearts (secretly, as per the rules).
5) West leads the Ace of hearts.
6) North makes her first error. She can trump it with the 10 of spades, but plays the 10 of diamonds. This is the worst possible play, but South won't discover this until later.
7) East follows suit with the Jack of hearts.
8) South must also follow suit with the King of hearts, and West wins the first trick.
9) West leads the Queen of hearts (this is a bad play, with three hearts in hand, but everything else is risky anyway).
10) North realizes her first play was poor, so she tries to make amends by trumping with the 10 of spades. South is, of course, amazed and disgusted.
11) East overtrumps with the Ace of spades, which upsets South even further.

12) Here, South has an awful choice. Play her low bower (the Jack of clubs), or forfeit another trick. South overtrumps with the low bower and wins the second trick. Tricks are tied 1-1.
13) South now has a King of spades and two high clubs. Because South started the game with three clubs, she's afraid that opponents will manage to take control on a void. So South leads the King of spades.
14) West plays the 10 of clubs, since all West's cards are terrible now.
15) Seeing this, North drops the Queen of clubs, and holds two diamonds: the Ace and Jack. This is a mistake a new player would make ... trying to make a void when there's no point, and forgetting that Jacks are worthless in the other colours.
16) East plays the Jack of spades and takes the third trick. Opponents lead 2-1.
17) East plays the King of diamonds ...
18) South has to play the King of clubs.
19) West follows suit with the 9 of diamonds.
20) North wins the trick with the Ace, and is very pleased with herself. South suddenly realises that North just discarded the Queen of clubs, and knows exactly what is about to happen.
21) North plays the Jack of diamonds.
22) East takes the last trick with the Queen of diamonds. South's Ace of clubs is worthless now.
23) West plays the 10 of hearts meaninglessly, and the dealer is euchred.

NOTES ON THE STORY

This play was Rob Winslow's idea. The piece I had written for the 4th Line Theatre had done pretty well and he wanted me to write another, maybe about one-room schools. So Rob—who knows that I'm drawn to stories about strong women—pointed out that in the old days, schoolteachers were often the only female professionals for miles around, and they must have some fascinating tales to tell (many fine teachers were men, but as I say, Rob knew who he was dealing with).

Later, Eric approached me to ask me about maybe writing for Blyth, and I proposed this play in the form of a question: "For more than a hundred years, all the children in a rural area passed through the same four walls. How much did the one-room school shape its community ... and how much did the community shape the school?" While I was in Suzanne Lebeau's playwright's unit at PWM (Playwrights Workshop Montreal)—where I began to write *Schoolhouse* in earnest—Paula Danckert kept asking me why I was writing this play, what it was really about ... and suddenly I knew. I said it would be, finally, a story about insiders and outsiders: about the fact that every time you draw a circle, some things are inside the circle, and some things aren't. I told them I wanted to look at the kind of place I had grown up in, and see what had shaped its values and what they were, and how people were cared for and accepted, and what happened when they were not.

And that's all I need to say about that.

NOTES ON PRODUCTION

Actually, when I went to Montreal, I was suffering from writer's block. Mostly, I was stymied by the question of how best to represent the children on stage. I wanted the world of the play to be presented with great warmth but without sentimentality; I needed performers with the innocence of little children, and the dramatic experience and comic timing of old pros; and I wanted the adults to be approached with the same honesty and lack of judgment as the children. So: should I be writing the play to be performed by children? Adults? Puppets? Some combination of the above?

As I shared this anxiety with the Québecois actors and writers who made up most of the PWM unit, they looked at each other in bewilderment. Finally, one of them said: "Mais ... c'est de la mise-en-scène, ça!" Which means (loosely translated): That's the director's problem!

Suddenly, I was free to write my story. And you, dear directors, actors, and other readers, are free to interpret it as you wish. Leah Cherniak's clown-influenced production showed the power of the imagination, with adult actors playing the children and then doubling, quite tellingly, as their own parents. Kim Blackwell's epic outdoor vision featured a cast of twenty, and benefitted from the simplicity and vulnerability of real children as the children. It is possible to do the play with as few as nine actors, or as many as twenty-two. I have yet to see the first all-marionette production, and I await it with some impatience.

One word of caution: I would be very, very reluctant to cast an actual fourteen-year-old as Ewart. Ewart not only looks much older than his age: he knows things that no fourteen-year-old should know. It's hard enough to find a young Melita who can ring all the changes, inhabit that world, and carry a show. Somewhere there may be a young boy with the sense of emotional damage (and the theatrical technique) to bring Ewart to the stage ... but I'd be a little scared to meet him. Go with the young-looking guy (or woman, or puppet) who can act, and you won't put a foot wrong.

ACKNOWLEDGEMENTS

As a playwright, the greatest blessing you can ever be given is a superb director who does her utmost to make your script work, and ruthlessly pinpoints exactly where it doesn't. Thanks to the gifted and generous Leah Cherniak and our exceptional cast, designers, and crew, this play got much better—and fourteen pages shorter. My deep gratitude belongs to them all, as well as to my beloved dramaturg, Christine Sumption of Seattle, for her clarity, good heart, and infallible diagnostic eye; to Suzanne Lebeau for understanding the hearts of children, and to Paula, Corey, and Playwrights Workshop Montreal for allowing us to meet; to Rob, Janette, Simone, Kim, and everyone at the 4th Line Theatre for their help, guidance, and long-term support of my work; and to Eric, Jane, and all at Blyth for their input, for the warm welcome they extended to me and my play, and for their crazy determination to help me put a whole village onstage. Also to Jovanni and my family and friends, for being my village.

Schoolhouse was commissioned by the Blyth Festival in 2004, with the aid of the the Ontario Council for the Arts, the Canada Council for the Arts, and the Laidlaw Foundation. The first draft was created in 2004-05 while I was OAC Playwright-in-Residence at the 4th Line Theatre. During this period, I was graciously hosted by Trent University's Champlain College, headed by Professors Stephen Brown and David Glassco. In March of 2005, I took three measly pages to the TYA Writers' Unit at PWM, facilitated by Paula Danckert and by Nadine Desrochers of CEAD and led by the amazing Suzanne Lebeau: I left with thirty-five pages and my two main characters. In April 2005, a partial draft was read at Trent University's Nozhem (First People's Performance Space) as part of 4th Line's Breaking Ground series of new work. The director was Robert Winslow. In August 2005, the play-in-progress received a public reading (as part of Blyth's Bonanza Weekend) and a workshop, both directed by Eric

Coates. Leah Cherniak directed a further reading for Blyth in May 2006. Those workshops were supported by the Roulston Roy New Play Development Programme. The following actors were part of the development process: Sarah Allen, Anne Anglin, Marie Beath Badian, Whitney Barris, Nancy Beatty, Joseph Bellerose, Cliff Cardinal, Adrian Churchill, Eric Coates, Danielle Desormeaux, Sylvain Dessureault, Waawaate Fobister, Gil Garratt, Henry Gauthier, Mark Harapiak, Justin Hiscox, Mark Hiscox, Renée Madeleine Leguerrier, Marika Lhoumeaux, Stephanie McNamara, Ken Munday, Lisa Norton, Phil Oakley, Michelle Pollak, Suzanne Roberts Smith, Patti Shaughnessy, Amy Jo Scherman, Erwin Weche, Janette Winslow, and Robert Winslow. I learned from each and every one of them.

This story cheerfully plunders the recollections of former one-room schoolteachers and students in the region of Millbrook, Ontario who were kind enough to share them with me (at a 4th Line Theatre Community Reminiscence, or individually). While this is a work of fiction, many of its incidents and characters came out of my interviews with these generous souls: Cameron Bonner, Glenna Brotherstone, Betty Brown, Edith Carr, Fraser Carr, Freda Eagleson, Gordon Eagleson, Margaret Eakins, Velma Fallis, Agnes Foster, Chester Froncz, Diane Froncz, Laverne Gibson, Marion Graham, Betty Joan Greer, Bob Greer, Ella Jones, Milburn Jones, Marilyn Kerr, Margaret Killeen, Larry Lamb, Marjorie Ludgate, Gail MacLaren, Mary MacLaren, Alec Macleod, Brenda McAdam, Marion Marvin, Gord Might, Irene Might, David Newhouse, Jean Olan, Annie Sharpe, Dorothy Stevens, Barb Stewart, Joyce Syer, Malcolm Syer, Bonna Todd, Dorothy Todd, Norma Warr, Doug Williams, and Ann Wylie. Special thanks to Milburn, Agnes, Barb, Fraser, Annie, Alex, Marjorie, Velma, and Cam—who must have been wonderful teachers—and to Eva Mary Bonner for organising a reminiscence at her home. Thanks to Loretta Merritt of Torkin Manes Barristers and Solicitors for information about the training school lawsuits; to Dean Gabourie for sharing his front-line social work experiences; and to Jonathan Sy, who co-designed the euchre game. I'd like to acknowledge the invaluable help of Johann Ramsaran, my research assistant, and of the Trent Centre for Community-Based Education, which put us together. Among many reference works, I am particularly indebted to Jean Cochrane's *The One-Room School in Canada*, which I heartily recommend to anyone interested in working on this play. All remaining errors and deficiencies are, of course, my own.

SCHOOLHOUSE (ALTERNATE SCENE)

Since the 4th Line is an outdoor theatre known for its use of real live-stock, Kim Blackwell wanted Dwight to have a live animal at the school fair. However, piglets, being far more intelligent creatures than calves, are much easier to handle. Accordingly, young Ophelia (and her companion and understudy, Hamlet) left a large industrial hog farm to join the company, and seemed to enjoy the attention immensely. Following in the footsteps of *Charlotte's Web*, I was happy to provide the words that gave these pleasant little creatures a new lease on life.

Here, then, is the altered section of Act I, Scene 12 (pp. 38–40):

Jericho School, November 1, 1938. MISS LINTON stands in front of the line of defendants: EWART, DWIGHT, FLOSSIE, and RUSSELL. The latter three are bandaged, plastered, and bruised. Silence.

MISS LINTON

Now. Who has an explanation as to why you three saw fit to lock a seven-year-old boy in the privy with a freshly butchered cow?

DWIGHT

Well, Dad told me for to go do somethin' with the head.

RUSSELL and FLOSSIE snicker, but MISS LINTON withers them with a look.

MISS LINTON

Let's try this again. Who has an intelligent explanation?

RUSSELL

It was just Hallowe'en, Teacher. We was just trying to scare him. It was all in fun.

MISS LINTON

Oh, good, Russell, I'm glad you explained that you were trying to scare him, because if I thought you were trying to behave like decent young people, I would be confused.

Beat: she changes tone completely.

By the way, Dwight, how's your pig?

DWIGHT

(*startled*) Do you mean me, Teacher?

MISS LINTON

Yes, I do. Your piglet that we saw at the school fair—that was a fine-looking animal—how's she doing?

DWIGHT

Well, Teacher, she's doing alright ... Now, mind, after the fair there she wouldn't eat nothin' and she was weavin' pretty good: I thought she might've got the blind staggers. So, that Mond'y I drenched her with bicarb and watched her all night for to see if her belly got hard, but turns out she just had a bit o' sunstroke.

MISS LINTON

Dwight Varnum, I suspect that that is the most you have ever said at one time in your life. Now why would you take such care with a baby pig? Do you love this pig? Is she a friend, would you say?

DWIGHT

I don't know, Teacher. You can't keep no hogs as a friend, it don't work out too good. Still, I raised her up pretty good, I guess, and she's a good little pig. I guess I feel all tied up with her.

MISS LINTON

So, you feel all tied up with minding a defenceless little beast but not with minding a defenceless little boy who needs your protection at least as much as that piglet does?

Beat.

You three don't like Milton, and there's not a blessed thing I can do about it. But you should know by now that someone smaller and frailer than you is someone you're supposed to look out for—the way the older children once looked out for you. So: today, at the end of class, I will escort you home to your parents, to tell them why you are suspended for one week.

There is consternation amongst the children ... .

96